C. K. BARRETT

The Signs of
an Apostle

THE CATO LECTURE 1969

With an Introduction
to the American Edition
by John Reumann

Fortress Press   Philadelphia

Published by Fortress Press, 1972

This book, *The Signs of an Apostle*, was first published by
Epworth Press, London, England, in 1970.
Copyright © C. K. Barrett, 1970.

INTRODUCTION TO THE AMERICAN EDITION
COPYRIGHT © 1972 BY FORTRESS PRESS

Library of Congress Catalog Card Number 72–75646

ISBN 0–8006–0116–5

3237B72   Printed in U.S.A.   1-116

Introduction to the

American Edition

by John Reumann

The Meanings of "apostle" and "apostolicity" compel attention historically and ecumenically today. Historically, no clear picture of primitive Christianity will ever emerge without settling, at least to a degree, who the apostles were and what they did (or did not do). Ecumenically, no solution is likely to be found for the current divided estate of Christendom without some attention to what apostolicity implies for the modern church.

The pages which follow, by Professor C. K. Barrett, of Durham University, England, originally presented as the Cato Lecture in Australia in 1969, give one scholar's calculated impression of what apostles were in the New Testament and what the "marks" therefore of apostolicity ought to be in the church. The larger portion of the book (pp. 23–81) represents historical analysis of the New Testament references to apostles, in light of the world of the day—Jewish background, Hellenistic practices, and gnostic and second-century developments. This survey—in terms the layman can follow, but based on over two decades of study and specialized publication by Professor Barrett—is preceded by a brief survey on some of the previous major works on the subject (especially pp. 12–16). The second part of the book (pp. 85–114) draws out implications for the apostolicity of the church today. Relevant reasons are given as to why the author has been drawn to consider "the authenticity of the church" in a "post-God-is-dead era" (pp. 17–20), and why at times his eye is on contemporary schemes of church reunion.

Professor Barrett writes for at least two types of readers. The one group is historically minded and wants to learn, in understandable terms, whither historical research has been tending with regard to apostles and Christian origins. The other group, ecclesiastically and ecumenically, is interested not in "what it meant" but in "what it means": What is an apostolic church today? The two interests are related, though results in each area can be judged separately, if one wishes.

Some of Professor Barrett's practical comments were made in light of the then impending Anglican–Methodist Scheme of Unity in the British Isles (see note 288). His views on such plans, as a "pooling of gifts" sometimes without regard for the basic truths of the gospel, are well known from articles elsewhere (see the bibliography, pp. 1–2). He has been critical especially of proposals which would mandate episcopacy and "apostolic succession" as essential to the ministry and church.

The reunion plan for the Church of England and the British Methodist Church, which grew out of negotiations over a twenty-year period, called for two stages: (1) full communion and integration of ministers, Methodists accepting the historic episcopate, by 1970; (2) organic union by 1980. A key feature was to be a "Service of Reconciliation" where "mutual recognition of ministries" was bestowed (seemingly acknowledging the "validity" of Methodist "orders") but with laying on of hands (seemingly validating Methodists at that moment). In a simultaneous vote on July 8, 1969, Methodists, meeting at Birmingham, approved the scheme with a 77 percent affirmative vote, but Anglicans at Westminster in effect defeated it in that only 69 percent approved, 6 percent under the required total. Attempts have been made to reconsider in 1972, but the fate of the proposal remains uncertain currently. One of the rocks on which the 1968 plan ran aground, in the opinion of Professor Barrett, who, as a Methodist clergyman, was involved in "The Voice of Methodism" against the scheme, was the question of apostolicity.

As a scholar of international stature in New Testament circles, Charles Kingsley Barrett needs little biographical introduction. Born in 1917, he studied at Cambridge (B.A., M.A., B.D., D.D.) and after serving as assistant tutor at Wesley College, Headingly, Leeds, and in a parish, began teaching in the theology faculty at Durham University, where he has been professor since 1959. He has been honored by fellow scholars in his selection as Deputy President-Elect of the Studiorum Novi Testamenti Societas, to succeed Ernst Käsemann in 1972–73. There are over a dozen books from his pen, including four commentaries.

Dr. Barrett has presented the Hewitt Lectures in 1961 on Pauline theology; the Shaffer Lectures at Yale in 1965, *Jesus and the Gospel Tradition*; and the Delitzsch Lecture in German, on the Fourth Gospel and Judaism (1970). He has contributed specialized studies on apostolicity to festschriften and other volumes from 1953 to the present, in Holland, Sweden, Germany, and Belgium, as well as in the British Isles. It is on these detailed treatments that he draws in setting forth many of the conclusions in *The Signs of an Apostle*. Because such articles are often quite technical and inaccessible, a summary of some of them is included in this Introduction, as are references to several monographs omitted because of limitations in time and space in the Cato Lecture (see p. 16).

There is a traditional picture of "twelve apostles," appointed by Jesus, with Peter exalted as leader, and Paul loosely linked with them as "the thirteenth apostle." Usually Paul's epistles, with their broader use of the term "apostle," have been read in light of the Lukan picture in Acts (where Paul is designated an apostle like "the twelve" only at 14:4 and 14). But recent critical studies have challenged the veracity of much in Acts. Many of these current critical views have been summed up and assessed by Professor Barrett's own handy little survey, *Luke the Historian in Recent Study*. He himself sees Luke as providing two pictures of the church: one, intentionally, of the first few decades, accurate or inaccurate, as his sources happen to be; the other, accidentally, of his own times and their views, superimposed on the first. In Barrett's opinion, Luke "had little knowledge" about apostles "apart from their number . . ." and "had no intention of magnifying them into religious dictators" (pp. 71 f.).

Günther Klein went further in his book on the idea of "twelve apostles" (1961), arguing that it was Luke who first gave the title "apostle" to "the twelve" and restricted the title to those twelve and no other. Klein suggests that Luke did this in order to preserve Paul for the church and make him unsuitable for gnostic claims: by denying Paul apostolic status and subordinating him to the twelve as a mere evangelist under the apostles, Luke is portraying a Paul to whom gnostics could not appeal over against church tradition.

Another major monograph, *The Office of Apostle in the Early Church*, by Walter Schmithals (1961; Eng. trans., 1969), deals with the origin of the concept "apostle." Secular Greek furnishes no real background. Jewish origins in the office of *shaliaḥ* (pp. 12–13 below) have not proven satisfactory.

Schmithals therefore suggests as background gnosticism, the "heavenly Apostle" who comes to earth as emissary with a call to awaken, and the earthly apostle as messenger of the heavenly emissary. Paul is said to have received his understanding of "apostle" from gnostic Christian circles in Syria, though he went on to develop his own particular notion of apostleship. Apostleship thus becomes a response by the church taken over from gnostic circles, rather than a creation by Christianity or the intention of Jesus. Professor Barrett has little to say directly about Schmithals's views (cf. his commentary on 1 Corinthians, p. v), but he consistently rejects any such background as well as Schmithals's contentions, in another book, about gnostic opponents in Corinth.

Important work on the nature of Paul's opponents in 2 Corinthians has been done by Dieter Georgi in a book in 1964 and by Gerhard Friedrich in an article (1963). Barrett has discussed, and in many ways rejected, these views in a paper in *New Testament Studies* (1971).

Georgi and Friedrich agree that the opponents of Paul in what we call 2 Corinthians were Hellenistic-Jewish Christians. For Georgi they are itinerant missionaries who have taken up ideas from the Hellenistic world, and who stress traditions concerning Moses and Jesus, and themselves as pneumatic, ecstatic, wonder-working, "divinized men" (*theioi andres*), "able" or "sufficient" for all things (3:5). Their letters of recommendation (3:1) and catch phrases—"seed of Abraham," "servants of Christ," "Hebrews, Israelites" (11:22–23)—dazzled the Corinthians and put into eclipse Paul's less sensational brand of apostleship which stressed life under the cross (1 Cor. 1:23, 4:9–13; 2 Cor. 11:24 ff.). Gladly the Corinthians supported, even financially (12:13), these "super apostles" (11:5, 12:11).

Friedrich sees them, not as *theioi andres* (Barrett agrees) but as from the Hellenist circle around Stephen (Acts 6–8). Barrett finds Stephen too shadowy a figure to posit behind the Corinthian situation. These varying views show how lively the subject is, and suggest that rival views of apostle can be found in the New Testament.

We now turn to Professor Barrett's own essays on apostleship. Running through them are certain common emphases. One is the idea of the apostle as an "eschatologic person." The phrase comes from the Swedish scholar Anton Fridrichsen, but the theme has been developed by Barrett, especially in a lecture at Uppsala, Sweden, in 1955. In "The Apostles in and after the New Testament" he suggests that the real problem is how an originally eschatological concept was "de-eschatologized" at the end of the first century. In many ways this remains the heart of the problem for the church: How can what was once vivid and dynamic, in light of an awareness that the ultimate had come and the final things were at hand, be sustained as the years roll by?

A second persistent feature in Barrett's studies is the endeavor to find roots not in mystery religions or gnosticism but in the Old Testament and the Christian gospel. Hence his opposition to Schmithals's supposed origins for the office of apostle. Already in a 1953 essay on apostles Barrett concluded that apostleship is to be illuminated by no other background than Christian eschatology. (Does that mean apocalyptic roots?) While noting history-of-religions backgrounds, Barrett is Bible-centered and specifically gospel-centered, in his interpretations.

Thirdly, attention must be called to a persistent view of Peter and the Jerusalem apostles as connected in some way with the troubles Paul faced in Galatia and Corinth.

Some exegetes distinguish, on the one hand, Peter, James, and John ("who were reputed to be pillars") and the troublemakers in Galatia on the other, usually referred to as Judaizers. Barrett senses that the authority of the Jerusalem pillars in the Jewish wing of the church was somehow being misused. But "eschatological office . . . in the last days" gives them "no exclusive rights" in the church, above all in Paul's Galatia. In Corinth, where Paul was the founding father of the congregation (1 Cor. 4:15), matters worsen. Peter seems to have visited there (9:5), and his Jewish-Christian opinions must have been something of an embarrassment for Paul. Later the situation deteriorates, under the impact of intruding Jewish-Christian missionaries, who are not gnostics or Hellenistic Jews (as Schmithals and Georgi or Friedrich claim), but "Jerusalem Jews, Judaizing Jews . . . a rival apostolate to Paul's, backed by all the prestige of the mother church" (*New Testament Studies* 17 [1970–71]: 251). Peter, though not mentioned by name in 2 Corinthians, looms as the menace to Paul's work there; a conservative "Petrine party" in Corinth may be the link between the troublemakers in 1 Corinthians and those in 2 Corinthians. Hence Barrett's judgment on Peter, in light of his analysis of the Corinthian situation and the earlier controversies in Galatia and at Antioch, where Paul had to rebuke Peter for failure to stand up for the gospel of freedom (cf. Gal. 2:12):

> Peter's heart was in the right place. . . . But he was easily frightened, and therefore easily influenced and used. More subtle and less scrupulous ecclesiastical politicians found him useful as a figure-head. Hence Paul's embarrassment. He could not simply repudiate Peter; yet Peter, in the hands of those who made use of him, was on the way to ruining Paul's work at Corinth. (*Abraham Unser Vater*, p. 12).

For Professor Barrett's fuller views we must await his commentary on 2 Corinthians (cf. his commentary on 1 Corinthians, p. 44).

The 1955 lecture, "The Apostles in and after the New Testament," is programmatic. After the New Testament, in the second century, the concept of apostle, Barrett maintains, was "de-eschatologized" along two lines. The one was gnostic. Here apostles were depicted as men who had accompanied the Savior on earth, but who, after Jesus' death, attained the new status of *theioi andres*, reborn men with a "divine spark" within, true gnostics who could confer the gift of regeneration or deification. The second line of development was Jewish and could either (a) take the form of the apostles being regarded as the starting-point for a chain of tradition, like rabbis, or (b) result in the virtual disappearance of apostles in favor of emphasis on the family of Jesus considered as priest-kings (cf. Eusebius, *Church History* 2.23.4; 3.20.1–8). By the turn of the first century the eschatological nature of apostles was no longer understood.

These later lines of development are foreshadowed in the New Testament. Originally, and clearly in Paul, apostleship was understood in an eschatological framework. But in Galatians 2 we see a different, "Jewish" understanding: the eschatological meaning of "pillars" is being modified so as to bolster up human authority. In the Corinthian letters we meet "super apostles" who stress authority and view themselves in Jewish and Hellenistic perspectives. Matthew's Gospel shows a tendency in 16:17 ff. to view Peter as prince of apostles, like a rabbi binding and loosing; but Galatians 2 could reflect this tendency carried to an extreme, so that Paul had to oppose it. The "pseudepigraphs" (Ephesians, the Pastorals, 1 Peter) view apostles as the beginning in a chain of tradition. John and Acts suggest apostleship means witnessing, in dependence upon the Spirit (a view unfortunately unstressed in the second century). Thus Barrett sees competing notions of apostleship in the New Testament.

Support for the interpretation given above of Galatians had been provided by Barrett's essay, "Paul and the 'Pillar' Apostles," published in 1953. The term "pillar" (Gal. 2:9), Barrett holds, is rooted in Old Testament and apocalyptic ideas of a "new temple." Since Jesus probably hoped for such a new temple in the age to come, it was natural for Jerusalem Christians to speak of their leading apostles as "pillars," who would occupy positions of importance in the new age. Paul too recognizes the eschatological role of these men, but because of the way the Judaizers are claiming certain rights institutionally on the basis of the pillars and their (eschatological) authority, Paul must qualify the term with the phrase " 'so-called' pillars" (2:9, "reputed"; cf. 2:2, 6a, 6c). In 1 Corinthians he must, in reaction, insist on Christ, not apostles, as foundation of the church and eschatological temple (1 Cor. 3:11, cf. 3:5 ff. and 3:16).

The Corinthian evidence is most fully explored in Barrett's Manson Memorial Lecture in 1963, and in his commentary on 1 Corinthians (1968). An essay in the Michel festschrift (1963) had examined all the possible references to Cephas (Peter) in the series of (four) Pauline letters to Corinth (especially 1 Cor. 1:12, 3:22, 9:5, 15:5; cf. 2 Cor. 10:7, 11:4, etc.). Barrett concludes Peter wielded considerable influence in Corinth and probably had visited there. His judgment as to the kind of person Peter was and what he stood for at this period has already been cited above. Although at the end of 1 Corinthians (15:11) Paul could still emphasize how he and Peter agreed on the resurrection of Jesus, the Corinthians had heard another type of apostolic preaching and

were familiar with an apostolic style that differed from
Paul's (9:5). Barrett thinks three or four parties had
arisen in Corinth: one attached to Peter (persons baptized by him or attracted to his positions); an Apollos-
party, stressing the "wisdom-method of preaching"; a
Pauline party that had developed in reaction; and probably a "Christ-party," more gnostic, that emerged in
opposition to the legalistic Peter-group. Barrett goes
further and endorses some of the suggestions advanced
by T. W. Manson (originally in the *Bulletin of the John
Rylands Library* 26 [1941]; reprinted in *Studies in the
Gospels and Epistles*, ed. Matthew Black [Philadelphia:
Westminster, 1962], pp. 190–209) which saw Cephas as
an interloper introducing Palestinian piety and Jewish
legalism into Corinth. Hence the name of Cephas slips
in at 3:22, as the real cause of schism, when Paul is
"rhetorically . . . off his guard."

By the time we come to 2 Corinthians, matters are
far worse. New troublemakers are at work. They are not
the same as the Christ-party at 1 Corinthians 1:12 but
stem from a delegation sent by the Jerusalem church and
its "superlative apostles" (2 Cor. 11:5, 12:11). These
troublemakers rely on traditions of their own and have
a different, Jewish-Hellenistic, view of apostleship. Barrett does distinguish the "false apostles" (11:13) from
this Jerusalem group, but sees the Cephas-party of 1
Corinthians as a link abetting the fresh difficulties. A
few passages in 2 Corinthians suggest this group of Jewish-Christian opponents at Corinth has a single leader
(cf. 10:7, a particular person who is confident that he
is Christ's; 11:4, someone who comes and preaches "another Jesus" [cf. Gal. 2 and 1:8 f.]). People rally round,
and glory in, this man's position (2 Cor. 5:12). Barrett
feels the very absence of the name Cephas in 2 Corinthians and the fact that the agreement of Galatians 2:7,

dividing the Mediterranean world into Petrine and Pauline spheres, has been flagrantly violated through Petrine activity at Corinth, point to the likelihood that Peter headed the mission of "super apostles" in Corinth! Small wonder Paul has little respect for the Jerusalem brand of *apostoloi* and downright opposition to their agents in Corinth.

In an essay on *pseudapostoloi* in the volume honoring the Belgian Catholic scholar Béda Rigaux (1970), Barrett examines in detail the singular reference at 2 Corinthians 11:13 to "false apostles, deceitful workmen, disguising themselves as apostles of Christ," like Satan himself. These men, according to Barrett, claim an office, apostleship, which they do not have, and exhibit moral perversity as well as doctrinal error in their message. While no exact Jewish parallels can be found for such charges and countercharges, the false apostles here are Judaizers, in Barrett's opinion, and the passionate feelings arise because Paul regards such perversion of the gospel as an eschatological phenomenon.

The clearest picture to date of Barrett's reconstruction of the situation in 2 Corinthians comes in his *New Testament Studies* article of 1971. Two groups of adversaries rivaling Paul are identified. Since the interaction of all three caused reconsideration of the Old Testament and the Jewish religion, they may be designated as three kinds of "Judaism." (1) The "pillars" or "super apostles" of Jerusalem, in that they kept the Christian faith in a Jewish framework, are a kind of "conservative Judaism" (not in the sense the term is used today). (2) The envoys of the Jerusalem church who appeared in Corinth both exaggerated the Judaism of those who sent them and adopted a veneer of non-Jewish, Hellenistic practices; they become "false apostles" who are neither good Jews anymore nor real Christians. They can be described as "liberal Judaism." (3) Paul himself represents "revolutionary Judaism." In many respects he remained a Jew (2 Cor. 11:22 ff.) but was indifferent to external features (1 Cor. 9:19–23); Christ alone, not the Law, is the center of his faith. "The future," Barrett concludes, "was Paul's," though always threatened by these rival views within the church.

The Corinthians had thus been confronted by competing understandings of the gospel, in the form of conflicting styles of apostolicity. They, alas, judged them on essentially Hellenistic grounds—the wrong criteria. Paul's plea is that apostolic life-style and preaching conform to the gospel of Christ crucified and its eschatology of "'already' but 'not yet' fully arrived" (1 Cor. 1:23; 4:8–13). At stake is the legitimacy of an apostle and of the gospel itself.

In saying that thus "theological conflict runs back into the origins of Christianity," Professor Barrett is claiming, of apostolicity, what Ernst Käsemann once suggested with regard to the canon of the New Testament:

> The New Testament canon does not, as such, constitute the foundation of the unity of the Church. On the contrary, . . . it provides the basis for the multiplicity of the confessions. . . . the Gospel is the sole foundation of the one Church at all times and in all places ("The Canon of the New Testament and the Unity of the Church" [1951], Eng. trans. by W. J. Montague in Käsemann's *Essays on New Testament Themes*, Studies in Biblical Theology, 41 [Naperville, Ill.: Allenson, 1964], pp. 103, 106).

Similarly, "apostolicity" does not constitute the foundation of the unity of the church, since it offers the basis for a multiplicity of "apostolicities"; it is the gospel alone which is the foundation of the church. Just as the New Testament canon is no unity itself but demands decision, both historically and theologically, as to what is primary or central, so too with apostolicity in early Christianity. It is not sufficient to affirm as a principle, or to be in favor of, an "apostolic church" or "apostolic doctrine" or "apostolic succession"—one must decide *which* apostolicity, *which* apostolic style, indeed *"which Jesus,"* set forth by rival groups who all claimed the title "apostle" in primitive Christianity, in order to arrive at "a sense of the center."

Professor Barrett's book at times lists very precisely the varied ways in which "apostle" is used in the New Testament (cf. below, pp. 39, 45 f., 71–73, 81). A good illustration of the current debate is found in the two contributions in *Dialog* magazine in 1969: Gerhard Krodel's article fully recognizes the diversity in the views of " (apostolic) ministry" found in the New Testament writings and the need to choose among them. Frank Senn's reply seeks a homogenizing use of "the whole of the canon." What current research forces us to on the "apostles question," I suspect, is to make some decisions ecumenically on what "apostolic" meant and means regarding message, life-style, and eschatology. "Apostolic" may not define the boundaries of the church; we may even have to choose among kinds of apostleship—Jewish, gnostic, "institutional," charismatic, or Pauline.

One final matter: the title of the book. "The signs of an apostle," as a phrase, derives from 2 Corinthians 12:12. It admirably suggests the twin interests of Professor Barrett's book: apostles and the marks of an apostolic church. But it is likely a phrase used by Paul's opponents who, in Hellenistic fashion, demand "signs" such as wonders, mighty works, and speaking in tongues. Professor Barrett is aware of all this, though inclined to attribute the phrase to the Corinthians themselves as one of their criteria, rather than to the opponents. He feels also that Paul "took it over and used it on his own account." To avoid confusion that would arise from different titles for British and American editions, the phrase stands. It admirably indicates the issue: *What* signs for apostolicity, *what* marks for the church? Those of the other New Testament apostles at Corinth or of Paul? The signs of "superlative apostles" and the "theology of glory" (see note 260) claimed by their agents, or the "theology of the cross" and of all "fools for Christ" (2 Cor. 12:11, 11:17)?

Lutheran Theological Seminary at Philadelphia
January 20, 1972

Selected Bibliography
for Further Reading

Books and Articles by C. K. Barrett

On Apostles and Related Topics (arranged chronologically; for details on many of them, see the Introduction to the American edition):

"Paul and the 'Pillar' Apostles." In *Studia Paulina in Honorem Johannis de Zwaan Septuagenarii*, pp. 1–19. Haarlem, Netherlands: De Erven F. Bohn, 1953.

"The Apostles in and after the New Testament." *Svensk Exegetisk Årsbok* 21 (1956): 30–49.

A Commentary on the Epistle to the Romans. Black's/Harper's New Testament Commentaries. London: A. & C. Black; New York: Harper & Row, 1957.

"Apostolic Succession" and "Apostolic Succession Again." *The Expository Times* 70 (1958–59): 200–202 and 330–31.

Luke the Historian in Recent Study. A. S. Peake Memorial Lecture, 6. London: Epworth, 1961. Reprinted with a new, select bibliography, Facet Books, Biblical Series, 24. Philadelphia: Fortress, 1970.

"Cephas and Corinth." In *Abraham Unser Vater: Juden und Christen im Gespräch über die Bibel, Festschrift für Otto Michel zum 60. Geburtstag*, edited by Otto Betz, Martin Hengel, Peter Schmidt, pp. 1–12. Arbeiten zur Geschichte des Spätjudentums und Urchristentums, 5. Leiden: Brill, 1963.

The Pastoral Epistles in the New English Bible, with introduction and commentary. The Clarendon Bible, 13. Oxford: Clarendon, 1963.

"Christianity at Corinth." Manson Memorial Lecture, Nov. 26, 1963. *Bulletin of the John Rylands Library, Manchester* 46 (March, 1964): 269–97.

A Commentary on the First Epistle to the Corinthians. Black's/Harper's New Testament Commentaries. London: A. & C. Black; New York: Harper & Row, 1968.

"Titus." In *Neotestamentica et Semitica: Studies in Honour of Matthew Black*, edited by E. Earle Ellis and Max Wilcox, pp. 1–14. Edinburgh: T. & T. Clark, 1969.

1

"*Pseudapostaloi* (2 Cor. 11.13)." In *Mélanges Bibliques en hommage au R. P. Béda Rigaux*, edited by Albert Descamps and André de Halleux, pp. 377–96. Gembloux, Belgium: J. Duculot, 1970.

"Paul's Opponents in II Corinthians." *New Testament Studies* 17 (1970–71): 233–54. Summary in *New Testament Abstracts* 16 (1971–72): 264 (reference cited by item number).

Other Important Books by C. K. Barrett mentioned in the Introduction:

The Holy Spirit and the Gospel Tradition. London: SPCK; New York: Macmillan, 1947. Paperback reprint, 1966.

Howard, W. F. *The Fourth Gospel in Recent Criticism and Interpretation.* Fourth ed. revised by C. K. Barrett. London: Epworth, 1955.

The Gospel according to St. John: An Introduction with Commentary and Notes on the Greek Text. London: SPCK; Greenwich, Conn.: Seabury, 1955.

The New Testament Background: Selected Documents. London: SPCK, 1956; New York: Macmillan, 1957. Paperback, Harper Torchbooks, 1961.

From First Adam to Last: A Study in Pauline Theology. The Hewitt Lectures, 1961. New York: Scribner's, 1962.

Biblical Problems and Biblical Preaching. Facet Books, Biblical Series, 6. Philadelphia: Fortress, 1964. Includes Barrett's inaugural address at Durham on eschatology.

Jesus and the Gospel Tradition. Philadelphia: Fortress, 1968.

Das Johannesevangelium und das Judentum. Franz Delitzsch Lecture, 19 (1967). Stuttgart: Kohlhammer, 1970.

BY OTHER AUTHORS ON THE
SUBJECT OF THIS BOOK

On Apostles and Apostleship:

MOSBECH, H. "Apostolos in the New Testament." *Studia Theologica* 2 (1949): 166–200.

KREDEL, E. M. "Der Apostelbegriff in der neueren Exegese." *Zeitschrift für katholische Theologie* 78 (1956): 169–93; 257–305.

SCHNACKENBURG, R. "L'apostolicité: état de la recherche." *Istina* (Paris) 14 (1969): 5–32. Summary in *New Testament Abstracts* 14 (1969–70): 654. Eng. trans., "Apostolicity: the Present Position of Studies," *One in Christ* (Sheffield) 6 (1970): 243–73.

GÜTTGEMANNS, E. "Literatur zur Neutestamentlichen Theologie: . . . IV. Mission, Verkündigung und Apostolat." *Verkündigung und Forschung* 12, Heft 2 (1967): 61–79.

ASHCRAFT, M. "Paul's Understanding of Apostleship." *Review and Expositor* 55 (1958): 400–412.

KLEIN, GÜNTHER. *Die zwölf Apostel. Ursprung und Gehalt einer Idee.* Forschungen zur Religion und Literatur des Alten und Neuen Testaments, 59. Göttingen: Vandenhoeck & Ruprecht, 1961.

SCHMITHALS, WALTER. *The Office of Apostle in the Early Church.* Eng. trans. by John E. Steely, from the German (1961). New York & Nashville: Abingdon, 1969.

———. *Gnosticism in Corinth: An Investigation of the Letters to the Corinthians.* Eng. trans. by John E. Steely, from the German (1956; ²1965). New York & Nashville: Abingdon, 1971.

ROLOFF, J. *Apostolat—Verkündigung—Kirche. Ursprung, Inhalt und Funktion der kirchlichen Apostelamtes nach Paulus, Lukas und den Pastoralbriefen.* Gütersloh: Gerd Mohn, 1965.

RIGAUX, BÉDA. "The Twelve Apostles." *Apostolic Succession: Rethinking a Barrier to Unity.* Concilium, vol. 34, pp. 5–15. New York: Paulist Press, 1968.

KRODEL, G. "Forms and Functions of Ministries in the New Testament." *Dialog* 8 (1969): 191–202. Summary in *New Testament Abstracts* 14 (1969–70): 296.

SENN, F. C. "Interpreting the Historical Development of Ecclesiastical Office." *Dialog* 8 (1969): 300–303. Summary in *New Testament Abstracts* 14 (1969–70): 655.

SCHÜTZ, J. H. "Apostolic Authority and the Control of Tradition: I Cor. xv." *New Testament Studies* 15 (1968–69): 439–57. Summary in *New Testament Abstracts* 14 (1969–70): 596.

KERTELGE, K. "Das Apostelamt des Paulus, sein Ursprung und seine Bedeutung." *Biblische Zeitschrift* 14 (1970): 161–81. Summary in *New Testament Abstracts* 15 (1970–71): 583.

BURCHARD, C. *Der dreizehnte Zeuge. Traditions- und kompositionsgeschichtliche Untersuchungen zu Lukas' Darstellung der Frühzeit des Paulus.* Forschungen zur Religion und Literatur des Alten und Neuen Testaments, 103. Göttingen: Vandenhoeck & Ruprecht, 1970.

3

HENNECKE, EDGAR. *New Testament Apocrypha*, edited by W. Schneemelcher. Eng. trans. edited by R. McL. Wilson. Vol. 2, *Writings Relating to the Apostles.* . . . Philadelphia: Westminster, 1965. See especially W. Schneemelcher, "Apostle and Apostolic," pp. 25–30; and W. Bauer, "The Picture of the Apostle in Early Christian Tradition," pp. 35–73.

On the Concept of "Divine Men" *(theioi andres)*:

VOTAW, CLYDE WEBER. *The Gospels and Contemporary Biographies in the Greco-Roman World.* Facet Books, Biblical Series, 27. Philadelphia: Fortress, 1970. Reprints 1915 essay, with introduction on problem and additional bibliography.

SMITH, MORTON. "Prolegomena to a Discussion of Aretalogies, Divine Men, the Gospels, and Jesus." *Journal of Biblical Literature* 90 (1971): 174–99.

GEORGI, DIETER. *Die Gegner des Paulus im 2. Korintherbrief: Studien zur Religiösen Propaganda in der Spätantike.* Wissenschaftliche Monographien zum Alten und Neuen Testament, 11. Neukirchen-Vluyn: Neukirchener Verlag, 1964.

FRIEDRICH, GERHARD. "Die Gegner des Paulus im 2. Korintherbrief." In *Abraham Unser Vater* (Michel festschrift, cited above), pp. 181–215.

New Testament Exegesis and Current Ecumenical Discussions:

SCHELKLE, K. H. *Discipleship and Priesthood.* Eng. trans. by J. Disselhorst from the German. New York: Herder & Herder, 1965.

BROWN, RAYMOND, S. S. *Priest and Bishop: Biblical Reflections.* Paramus, N.J.: Paulist Press, 1970.

HANSON, R. P. C. *Groundwork for Unity: Plain Facts about the Christian Ministry.* London: SPCK, 1971. The (Anglican) Bishop of Clogher here stresses, in light of current ecumenical debate about the ministry, the need to reflect recent critical study of Christian origins.

On the Plan for Anglican/Methodist Unity:

"Ecumenical Calamity." *The Christian Century* 86 (July 23, 1969): 969.

MARTIN, CHRISTOPHER. "Anglican–Methodist Union: Past and Perspectives." *Journal of Ecumenical Studies* 7 (1970): 188–94.

TURNER, BRYAN S. "The Sociological Explanation of Ecumenicalism." *The Expository Times* 82 (1970–71): 356–61, especially 360–61.

See also the documents cited in note 288 and in the Introduction to the American edition.

Preface

THE FIRST PURPOSE of this Preface is to thank the administrators of the Cato Lecture, and the General Conference of the Methodist Church of Australasia, for inviting me to give the lecture at the Brisbane Conference in 1969; its second purpose is to thank those innumerable Australians who made my wife and me so welcome, and gave us six of the happiest weeks of our lives. To list their names would be impossible; if one may stand for all, let me name C. K. Daws, who from 1966 to 1969 was Secretary-General of the Methodist Church in Australasia, and at the Conference of 1969 became its President-General. If in the eighteen months before the lecture he sometimes had me worried, in the end all his planning was justified in perfect execution. And far beyond his administrative skill went his friendship, and his apprehension of the theological and ecclesiastical potential of the lecture so wisely and generously endowed by the late Fred J. Cato.

The third purpose of the Preface is to say a word about the printed form in which the lecture, delivered orally on 16 May 1969, now appears. The preparation of this little book has caused me great perplexity. One thing is clear to me. I cannot put out of my mind the vast crowd that thronged the church, and overflowed it, that warm May evening. I did my best to speak to them, and I wish to write for them now. At the same time I cannot forget my obligation to the professional theologians of Australia, the ministers and the students of theology. It is not easy to combine two purposes in one book; not easy, but I hope not impossible, if my readers will be tolerant of one another, as well as of me. I have left many things out; for example, I intended to include a much fuller account of recent study of the apostles than I have in fact given; for this, perhaps, my apologies are due mainly to the scholars I have failed to quote at length. I can assure them that their work has been pondered carefully, and has helped me much, even when I have not agreed with it. And I have provided a large number of notes. I hope that those who are not interested in theological technicalities will tolerate these in the interests of those who are; and that the latter will forgive me for relegating to notes what might well have stood in the text. Some of the notes, I should add, are designed to help the layman with information that the professional will already possess.

The reader will find what I said at Brisbane on pp. 11, 16–20, 35–44, 76–81, 85–96, 103 f., 108–10, 112, 113. This is the essence of what I want to say in this book, and if he finds some of the detail forbidding he may well begin with these pages.

So far I have spoken only of Australia. The same tour that took me, lecturing and preaching, from Perth round about (as Paul might say) as far as Cairns, carried me on to New Zealand and Fiji. In these countries also the Cato Lecture was heard, and the same warm-hearted hospitality, which never failed to include a sharing of the things of mind and spirit, was displayed. For this we have the same gratitude to express.

One thing more. The latter part of this book, which deals with the apostolicity of the church, contains here and there specific judgements on issues of current church debate. I should like, but cannot allow myself, to think it superfluous to point out that these judgements rest upon the exegetical work of the first part, and not vice versa. If the exegesis is false, the judgements will fall to the ground; it it is true, they will at least have to be taken seriously. But it is in the exegesis that the issue lies, and what I have said I now print in the hope that it may not be too late to be of use in Australia.

Durham   C. K. BARRETT
September 1969

THE FRED J. CATO LECTURESHIP

IN RESPONSE to an offer made by Mr Fred J. Cato to provide the endowment for a lecture that should be an original contribution to Theology, and of interest and value to Australasian Methodism, 'the Fred J. Cato Lectureship' was founded by the General Conference of the Methodist Church of Australasia at its triennial meeting in Sydney, May 19, 1932.

The lecturer shall be a representative Methodist Minister or Layman, preferably from Great Britain, to be selected by the General Conference or by a Committee of the same, and he shall deliver the lecture or a synopsis thereof during the sessions of the General Conference. The Publication of the lecture shall be subject to the following conditions:

(a) That the subject matter of the lecture shall not have been previously published.

(b) That it shall subsequently be published to the satisfaction of the Committee.

'Mr Cato's desire and purpose were to enrich the life and thought of the Australasian Methodist Church and to encourage and foster fraternal relations with Methodism of other lands.'

Contents

Introduction

A LECTURER who is given complete freedom in the choice of his topic may reasonably be expected to begin by explaining his subject, and why he has chosen it. Three reasons have led me to this one.

The first is that during the last twenty years or so a number of important discussions of the role of the apostles in the New Testament have been published. Some of them have undoubtedly made great positive contributions to the subject, and will have lasting value; some of them seem to me to be somewhat perverse and wrong-headed – the authors of these will no doubt think me perverse and wrong-headed; all of them are, in different ways, suggestive and thought-provoking. They have the effect of bringing the historical figures of the apostles, or, if this is preferred, the non-historical concept of apostleship, into relation with the issues of New Testament theology that press with some urgency upon our generation. This conjunction of the historical (or quasi-historical) and the theological in the person of the apostles is less striking and central than the same conjunction in the person of Jesus of Nazareth, but no one who is concerned about the history and theology of the earliest church can afford to neglect this aspect of its life, or these recent discussions of it.

To these discussions I shall refer occasionally in the

following pages. As I have pointed out in the Preface (p. 6), it was at first my intention to include at this point in the printed version of the lecture an account of the progress of research into the question; this intention I have abandoned because such an account, necessarily tedious to all but professional students, might have led some who, I hope, will read this book to feel that it was not for them. The expert will certainly know the story at least as well as I do, and will therefore, I hope, feel no great loss. It may, however, be useful at least to mention a few important names.

The foundation, or point of departure, for most modern studies was set out before the second world war by K. H. Rengstorf in a book, *Apostolat und Predigtamt*,[1] and in the article on *apostle* (ἀπόστολος) in Kittel's *Theologisches Wörterbuch zum Neuen Testament*.[2] Rengstorf was not the first scholar[3] to draw attention to the parallel between *apostle* and the rabbinic term *shaliaḥ* (or *shaluaḥ*), but he was the first to make full, accurate, and systematic use of it. It is laid down (for example, in Berakoth 5.5) that 'a man's agent [*shaliaḥ*] is like to himself'; the agent's acts implicate his principal. Thus, in the Mishnah quoted:

If he that says the *Tefillah* falls into error it is a bad omen for him; and if he was the agent of the congregation[4] it is a bad omen for them that appointed him, because a man's agent is like to himself.

This proposition is by no means peculiar to Judaism. T. W. Manson,[5] for example, quotes the familiar legal tag, *qui facit per alium facit per se*; but the parallel between the Greek word (ἀπόστολος) and the Hebrew (*shaliaḥ*, *shaluaḥ*), both meaning 'one who has been sent', together with the fact that the events of early Christianity were played out against a Jewish background, give the rabbinic saying special relevance.

What is its relevance?

In this way the essence of the apostolic consciousness of office and of vocation is uniquely disclosed. It is based upon the certainty that one has been so appropriated to Christ as to represent him in one's own person, and in the fact that he has taken into his hands the whole life of the officebearer.[6]

For Rengstorf the important points are that an apostle's dignity and worth lie not in himself but in the one who sends him; that the sending must be a personal sending by Jesus of a man who has been in personal contact with him; that the chief work of an apostle is the proclamation of a message; that the apostle acts with authority, and that his message and his actions are bound up with each other; that the apostle shares not only in the authority but also in the suffering of the Lord.

The *shaliaḥ*-institution, and the principle that 'a man's agent [*shaliaḥ*] is as the man himself', have been employed in various ways that can hardly be cleared of the charge of special pleading. Thus it is used by Gregory Dix in his (in some ways profound and stimulating) essay in *The Apostolic Ministry*[7] as the basis of the doctrine of apostolic succession.

The element of continuity, the permanent creative germ which makes all these stages essentially phases of one and the same organic process, and not a series of new administrative devices to meet new conditions, is the personal commission of the *shaliach* to act in the Person of our Lord

Himself, conveyed afresh to individuals in every generation by Him acting through other individuals who have already personally received that commission to act in His Person. When they so act, using the ancient Jewish gesture, He Himself cannot repudiate their action; another *shaliach* is made. 'For a man's *shaliach* is as it were himself.' (p. 287)

It is worth noting in passing that, though the Jewish institution is not without value in the study of Christian origins, it cannot mean what Dix suggests. Even if it could, a saying from the Mishnah would be an odd foundation for the Christian ministry; but in fact it was outside the competence of a *shaliaḥ* to create a further *shaliaḥ*. This is shown by T. W. Manson,[8] who once more has the appropriate legal tag to sum up the point: *delegatus non potest delegare*.

An analogous use of the *shaliaḥ* material is made by J. N. Geldenhuys,[9] who seeks by means of it to prove not only the authority but also, in a literal sense, the inerrancy of Scripture. The Lord himself was possessed of complete divine authority; he transferred authority to those whom he appointed as his *shᵉluḥin* (agents), and they exercised it, in preaching, in founding churches, and in the literature for which they were responsible. Undoubtedly there is truth in this presentation of the matter; but not only is it set out in too mechanical a way, it fails to do justice to historical facts about the apostles that will be noted below.[10]

It would not be proper for me to blame Dix and Geldenhuys for drawing practical conclusions; I shall do something of the sort myself in the latter part of this book. They may, however, be criticized for having rushed the essential work of history, and leapt too quickly, on the basis of the apparently convenient *shaliaḥ* passages, to conclusions that lean too heavily on the Mishnah and do less than justice to the New Testament. The true line of descent from Rengstorf is given not by those who have sought to make quick and easy capital out of his results but by those who have continued the historical inquiry.

A. Fridrichsen[11] took the important step of insisting that the theme of apostleship is to be set in the context of that eschatological way of thinking that forms the framework of New Testament theology. 'When Paul in Romans introduces himself as a κλητὸς ἀπόστολος [one called to be an apostle] he characterizes himself as an eschatologic person' (p. 3). The particular 'Gospel' entrusted to him made him in particular an apostle to the Gentiles: this was his role in the working out of God's purpose. This observation is reflected in three important papers contributed to the Scandinavian series *Studia Theologica* – by H. von Campenhausen,[12] who goes on to deal with the question of apostolic authority, and the canon of the New Testament; by H. Mosbech,[13] who develops the question (also discussed by von Campenhausen) of the historical origins of the apostolate and the relations between the various persons described in the New Testament as apostles; and by J. Munck,[14] who brings out the different conceptions of apostleship represented in the New Testament, and especially the relation between Paul's conception and that which prevailed elsewhere.

Articles such as these laid bare a variety of complex historical questions. Who were the apostles? the Twelve only? the Twelve together with Paul? But if the number twelve is exceeded, must not other additions be made as well as Paul? Were there more kinds of apostle than one – perhaps apostles of Christ, and also apostles of churches (2 Cor. 8: 23)? If there were several kinds of apostle, were there also different notions of what apostleship meant? If so, can these be distinguished, and their relations and intermingling determined? Two books in particular have dealt with these questions, G. Klein's *Die zwölf Apostel: Ursprung und Gehalt einer Idee*,[15] and W. Schmithals's *Das kirchliche Apostelamt: Eine historische Untersuchung*.[16] These books bear the same date, and are to a considerable extent independent, though Klein had the advantage of seeing Schmithals's typescript, and Schmithals saw Klein's book in time to be able to write an eight-page appendix of comments on it.

This body of literature[17] invites discussion from the student of early Christian history, but, for reasons I have already mentioned, in this lecture, or little book, the discussion will have to be implicit rather than explicit; and not a few of the questions raised will not be discussed at all.

The second factor that leads me to the subject of apostles and apostolicity is in part a personal one, and for that reason I hesitate to mention it; it is, however, too important, objectively as well as personally, to omit. For several years now – and it will be true for several years to come – my own attention has been focused within the New Testament on the Epistles to the Corinthians and the Acts of the Apostles. To anyone who is familiar with these books I need not say that their contents – and those of the Epistles at least as much as those of Acts – point to the question of apostleship. I must not linger over the matter here, for we shall meet it in some detail later; perhaps it

can be best – at least, most provocatively and paradoxically – indicated by setting out side by side two of
Paul's propositions, both drawn from 1 Corinthians:

There are some whom God has set in the church, first
apostles (12: 28);
I think God has put on us the apostles as last in the show
(4: 9).

No one can read the documents I have mentioned
without facing the questions: what is an apostle? what
sort of figure does he cut? what is his role in the
church? Nor, in this context, can he face these questions
without further wondering whether Paul and Luke
answer them in the same way. And when he is done
with the historical questions he will hardly avoid the
practical question: what, then, is an apostolic ministry?

It is easy to pass from the questions I have just
stated to the third consideration that has led me to my
subject, though this must be formulated in terms not
of the history of the first century but of the circumstances
of the church in the twentieth. We are confronted today
in a variety of ways with the question of the authenticity
of the church. What I mean by this term can be brought
out best by concrete examples, which I shall mention
now as questions, and in the greatest brevity, because I
shall return to them in due course.

First, there is preaching. I need not argue, for we
are all agreed, that those who are responsible for the
church's proclamation must be familiar with the
environment of thought and life in which the proclamation takes place. If we do not speak in a language,
and in an idiom of thought as well as speech, that our
hearers can understand, we might as well keep silence.

Nor is this simply a matter of accommodation in language, of intelligibility; a Christian has no right to make up his mind in advance that there is nothing he can learn from non-Christian thinkers. The Bible itself is a record of the appropriation of secular language and secular thought-forms for the expression of particular biblical truth. But where does this process end? When does Christian preaching become so thoroughly accommodated to its non-Christian environment that it ceases to be Christian? It is easy to feel that some have gone too far, easy too to understand why others have reacted against such excess and withdrawn into a Christian esotericism unintelligible to those who have not been brought up on the Bible, and in consequence almost worthless in evangelism. It is easy to recognize, and indeed to sympathize with, both these errors; far harder to define precisely the right course to follow. What are the criteria by which this course may be determined? What is the authentic Christian message, challenging and offensive, yet intelligible and ultimately credible?

What I have said about preaching could equally be said about dogmatics, which is the critical process by which the church's proclamation is regulated.[18] Again, brevity is best achieved by reference to extremes. The present decade has heard the proposition, 'God is dead'. This may be the passing oratorical fantasy of a popular preacher, determined to shake up his congregation at any price; perhaps it simply does not mean, and was not intended to mean, what it says, in which case it is best not used by serious people; taken at face value, it is a statement that negates and destroys Christian truth. Yet, when all this has been said – and it needs to be said – it is also true that a dogmatic that is not radically critical, and a Christology that does not do full justice to the problematical evidence of the New Testament documents as this appears in the light of modern scholarship, are not worth consideration. We have a great deal to learn from the past, and would-be theologians who cannot take the trouble to learn it are only playing at their profession; yet we cannot today simply repeat like parrots the documents either of the fifth century or of the sixteenth. To do this would be to shirk our responsibilities and run away from the question that challenges us as uncomfortably and as uncompromisingly as it challenged any of our fathers: what is authentic Christian doctrine, and where shall we find it?

The question of the authenticity of the church is raised again by the closer relations which today exist between the several denominations of Christians. It is hard to see how any Christian can do anything but rejoice in these closer and warmer relations, but they also have the effect of raising new questions, or rather, perhaps, of bringing new urgency into old questions. Is there any form of the church that can claim, beyond all others, to be authentically Christian, so that in unions between denominations this form must take precedence, and determine the structure of a united church? I am not speaking here simply about the rival claims of independency, presbytery, and episcopacy; this question is important enough, but there are others that run deeper still, and unity discussions have often tended to remain on the surface, and to be content with political trading. Is the church in its authentic being hieratic, hierarchical, sacerdotal? is it, and must it be, an institution, and must the institution be marked by exclusiveness and continuity? Or is it what some would call a 'lay' body, with institutions its grave, and ceremony its winding-sheet? In other words, is a particular form given with and inseparable from the substance of the church, so that wherever the church truly, and fully, exists, this form must appear, serving as a necessary mark of the authentic church? Or is the church free to develop forms, or to dispense with them, as from time to time it sees fit, so that no form but freedom from form proves to be the mark of its authenticity? Or will neither of these simple alternatives meet the requirements of the situation?

These are questions of some urgency, but we are not yet in a position to answer them. Our first duty is to observe that they exist, and that they demand answers. In our generation the church has sometimes been too ready to talk loosely about 'mission' without seriously raising the question what Gospel it intends to preach, too ready to rush into reunion schemes without observing the implications of the order to which it thereby commits itself. It is not enough to call ourselves 'the church'; the title is meaningless if we are not the church of Jesus Christ, which we know (as we know him) only through the apostles. That is, authenticity is apostolicity,[19] and we return, by way of the apostolicity of the church, to our first question: who were the apostles?

The Apostles in the

New Testament

The Apostles in the
New Testament

THE QUESTION, Who were the apostles? may well
seem too elementary to discuss on a serious occasion.
It is natural to reply: We know well who the apostles
were; we have read their names and their record
repeatedly in the gospels and in the Acts. Whether the
question is as easy as appears on the surface may perhaps
be doubted. We may, however, begin where the common sense of the average man would suggest, though
it may be that later we shall see reason to make a new
beginning elsewhere.[20]

In Mark, the earliest gospel, there is a list of twelve
names; it will not be superfluous to recall it (3: 16–19):
Simon (who receives the name 'Peter', 'Rock'); James
and John the sons of Zebedee (who receive the name
'Boanerges', 'Sons of Thunder'); Andrew; Philip;
Bartholomew; Matthew; Thomas; James the son[21] of
Alphaeus; Thaddaeus; Simon the Cananaean;[22] Judas
Iscariot. Of other disciples only one is named in Mark:
Levi the son[23] of Alphaeus, whose call is described in
2: 14,[24] though an undefined group of disciples
(μαθηταί) is fairly frequently mentioned.[25] When we
turn to the Matthaean parallel (10: 2ff.), we find slight
variations in order,[26] though Matthew now acquires
the title, 'the tax-collector', and correspondingly in
Matt. 9: 9 the Marcan Levi becomes Matthew. Were

Levi and Matthew the same person? Mark did not think so, and we may suppose that the first evangelist used the traditional story of the call of a tax-collector in the interests of one of the Twelve. That the one of the Twelve singled out for this description is Matthew, and that Matthew accordingly takes the place of Levi, is very probably to be connected with the traditional ascription of the first gospel to Matthew, but the sources hardly permit us to go further than this unadventurous comment. In Luke also (6: 14ff.) most of the Marcan names recur, and Levi is still Levi. Up to James the son of Alphaeus there is no difference except in order. Then follows Simon the Zealot,[27] Judas the son[28] of James (replacing Thaddaeus), and Judas Iscariot. So far no serious problem arises, since a case can be made out[29] for regarding Thaddaeus (and Lebbaeus, which appears as a textual variant for Thaddaeus)[30] as adjectival complements attached to the proper name Judas. Even if this case is not regarded as convincing – and it is far from conclusive – and we have to acknowledge that there is at this point a real difference between the Marcan and Lucan lists, such a difference is not at all surprising, and no more than might be expected in the circumstances. It should, however, be remembered when the origin of the Twelve and of traditions about them is considered;[31] and so should the occurrence of Judas Iscariot in all the synoptic lists.

The twelve, as a group, are referred to in John (6: 67, 70, 71; 20: 24), but there is no list of their names. Simon Peter, Andrew, the sons of Zebedee (but without the personal names 'James' and 'John'),[32] Philip, Thomas, Judas Iscariot, and a Judas not Iscariot (14: 22), who may be Luke's Judas son of

James, are mentioned; Bartholomew, Matthew, Levi, James the son of Alphaeus, Thaddaeus (and Lebbaeus), and Simon the Cananaean (or Zealot),[33] are not. A few other disciples are named or alluded to in significant ways. Most important is the 'disciple whom Jesus loved' (13: 23; 19: 26; 20: 2; 21: 7, 20), who is often, but not certainly, identified with John the son of Zebedee.[34] This disciple is referred to in 21: 24 as the author of the gospel, or at least of part of it, and is probably referred to in 19: 35 as the trustworthy witness. It is much harder to identify him with the 'other disciple' of 18: 15, and with the unnamed partner of Andrew in 1: 35–40. Lazarus, the brother of Mary and Martha,[35] is mentioned in 11: 1–44; 12: 1,9; and Nathanael at 1: 45. Nicodemus is hardly a disciple at 3: 1; 7: 50; but when he reappears at 19: 39 it is in company with Joseph of Arimathaea, who, according to John (19: 38), was a secret disciple. That John possessed traditions independent of those used by the other evangelists, which could account for the appearance of a few fresh names, would be agreed by most students; it is in fact striking that the fresh names are so few. It is not surprising that John retains the notion of 'the Twelve'; by the time he wrote they had become ineradicably fixed in the tradition. A familiar Jewish tradition (Sanhedrin 43a), according to which Jesus had five disciples, Mathai, Nakkai, Netzer, Buni, and Todah, is in this respect more interesting. It would be rash to base historical reconstruction upon it, but it may lend some weight to the view that traditions about 'the Twelve' have been formalized in Christian circles, and that the theological significance found in the number was more influential than personal recollection of a group whose members happened to add up to twelve.

It will be noted that so far we have, following the example of many New Testament passages,[36] spoken simply of the Twelve, without supplying any noun with the numeral. The Twelve appear, as a group that needs no further definition, as early as 1 Cor. 15:5, and two features of the gospel material go far to confirm the historicity of the tradition: first, the fact that so many of the names of those who make up the group are mere names – the number goes further and more definitely back into tradition than do the persons; and second, the persistent tradition[37] that Judas Iscariot was 'one of the Twelve' – the picture of a traitor in the inner circle is not one that would be lightly invented.

In one saying only, but that probably an old one,[38] the number finds explicit interpretation. This occurs in:

Matt. 19:28:

Verily I tell you, that you who have accompanied me, in the regeneration, when the Son of man sits on his glorious throne, you yourselves also shall sit upon twelve thrones, judging the twelve tribes of Israel.

Luke 22:28ff.:

You are those who have stayed with me in my trials; and as my Father convenanted to me a kingdom, so I covenant to you that you may eat and drink at my table in my kingdom, and you shall sit upon thrones judging the twelve tribes of Israel.

In both forms of this saying there are marks of editorial handling. The 'kingdom of the Son of man,' or 'of Jesus' is a later formula than 'kingdom of God' (or 'of heaven'); Matthew's 'regeneration' ($\pi\alpha\lambda\iota\gamma\gamma\epsilon\nu\epsilon\sigma\acute{\iota}\alpha$) is a word of his own, and Luke's reference to eating and drinking reflects his placing of the saying at the Last Supper. But common to the two is the contrast between the sufferings which the Twelve share with Jesus during his ministry, and the glory they will share with him afterwards. This contrast belongs to one of the earliest strata of the gospel tradition, and carries with it, with some degree of probability, both the Twelve as a body, and the interpretation of them as the judges of the twelve tribes of Israel, that is, as the rulers of the newly reconstituted people of God in the last days. It is not probable that this belief was read back from the rule of the Twelve in the early days of the church in Jerusalem,[39] if only because the Twelve appear to have played no significant part there.[40] That the Twelve originated in the setting of Jesus' understanding of his ministry in terms of present obscurity and suffering and future glory is confirmed by the names applied to outstanding members of the group: Simon becomes Peter, the Rock;[41] James and John, Boanerges, the Sons of Thunder.[42] These names have often been given moralizing interpretations. These are almost certainly mistaken. Simon was anything but rocklike, not only during the ministry of Jesus but afterwards too,[43] and there is very little evidence (possibly Luke 9: 51-6) to connect the characters of James and John with a thunderstorm. The names are eschatological:[44] Peter is the rock that will stand up to the storms of the last days, over which the gates of Hades, the power of death, will not prevail; James and John are the claps of thunder that herald the coming storm.

It is worth while to collect this additional evidence, for it suggests that the group of Twelve was neither an after-Easter phenomenon read back into the time of

Jesus, nor a piece of secondary mythology, created on the basis of the number that represented the totality of the people of God. The slight fluctuation in the list of names suggests that the make-up of the group may not have been completely invariable. There is variation in the inmost circle: sometimes Andrew appears with Simon, James, and John,[45] sometimes he does not. It would not be surprising if there were some variation in the next circle too; nor is it surprising that out of a wider group of adherents twelve should stand closer to Jesus than the rest, and three or four closest of all. They were not an *élite*, made up of the outstandingly virtuous, pious, and intelligent; they were the babes to whom the mystery, too simple to be worthy of the attention of the wise and prudent, was given (Matt. 11:25; Luke 10:21). Their one merit was that they stood with Jesus (Mark 4:10). His mission was to all Israel,[46] but it was the common people, to whom he had committed himself (e.g. Mark 2:17; Luke 19:10), who heard him gladly (Mark 12:37). Whether Jesus ever gave up the hope of winning the allegiance of all Israel it would be hard to say – Matt. 23:37ff. (= Luke 13:34f.) may suggest that he did; at all events the Twelve were the firstfruits, the nucleus of the new people, and, as such, they were exposed, with him, to the apocalyptic terrors that the doomed forces of evil would in their death throes bring upon the world.

Where the Twelve appear without further designation it is natural to supply the noun 'disciples'. The phrase 'twelve disciples' appears explicitly only in Matt. 10:1; 11:1; and possibly also in 20:17 and 26:20, though here readings differ; but it is fair to say that it is implied by some Marcan passages, for example:

Mark 9: 31, 33, 35:

He was teaching his disciples ... they came to Capernaum
... he called the Twelve ...

Mark 10: 32:

They were going up to Jerusalem ... those who followed
were afraid ... he took the Twelve ...

And the account (Mark 3: 14) of the appointment of
the Twelve implies selection out of a larger group of
disciples.[47] It would of course be absurd to think that
the Twelve were not learners, though Matthew's special
interest (cf. 28: 19) may be discerned in his emphatic
use of the word 'disciple'.

We return directly to our own theme when we ask if
the Twelve were also apostles. Mark uses the word once
only, at 6: 30 when the Twelve return from the mission
on which they have been sent. Here the word is simply
a verbal noun, with no necessary implications about a
specific status or office: Those who had been sent[48]
returned. Matthew also uses the word once only, at
10: 2. Here it is clear that Matthew is not reproducing
traditional material but simply providing his own
editorial setting for the traditional list of names: The
names of the twelve apostles were as follows. This
sentence shows that when Matthew wrote his book the
Twelve were known as apostles; but this was not in
doubt, and what we wish to know is whether they were
already apostles, and were already known as apostles,
during the ministry of Jesus. The word 'apostle' occurs
six times in Luke. Luke 9: 10 reproduces Mark 6: 30
and invites the same comment. Luke 17: 5; 22: 14;
24: 10 are Luke's own editorial stage directions and
therefore reflect the usage of his own time, not

necessarily that of the ministry of Jesus: The apostles said to the Lord; the apostles sat down with him; they told the apostles. This leaves two Lucan passages:

Luke 11: 49:

For this reason the wisdom of God said: I will send them prophets and apostles, and they will kill and persecute some of them, . . .

We can make little of this verse. The parallel (Matt. 23: 34: For this reason, behold I am sending you prophets and wise men and scribes; and you will kill and crucify some of them, . . .) preserves in some but not all respects an earlier form of the saying.[49] The reference to wisdom is probably original, but the word 'apostles' probably represents Luke's Christianizing application of the wisdom saying. If, however, the word is thought original it should, with T.W. Manson,[50] be rendered 'messenger':

The term 'apostles' has a technical ecclesiastical sense, which ought not to be read into the text here. Jesus used the Aramaic equivalent of the word, and – as I think – gave it as a name to certain of his disciples; but he used it in a wide sense to designate anyone who had a mission from God to men.

Manson's words lead us to the remaining Lucan passage, as the only piece of verbal evidence by which Manson's own conclusion could be firmly supported.

Luke 6: 13:

He chose out of his disciples twelve, whom he also named apostles.

In fact this verse does not support Manson's view that

Jesus called some of his disciples 'messengers' (shᵉluḥin), for Luke's 'whom he also named apostles' is simply his equivalent for Mark's 'that he might send them out to preach' (3: 14).[51] Luke is following Mark, and these Marcan words have no equivalent except the clause before us.

Behind the verbal question whether or not Jesus (or even the earliest tradition) described the Twelve as envoys, messengers, apostles (ἀπόστολοι, shᵉluḥin) is a much more important set of historical questions. Did Jesus, with or without the use of the word, appoint the Twelve with a view to sending them out as envoys (as Mark 3: 14 explicitly states that he did)? Did they take part in a mission to Israel during the ministry of Jesus (as Mark 6: 12f. explicitly states that they did)? Did they do so subsequently, after the death and resurrection of Jesus? Whatever answers be given to these questions, a further question lurks behind them; we are far from ready to answer it, but it will be well to pose it explicitly: How, and through whom, did the church's mission to the Gentile world begin?

It is worth while to put these questions together, because they help to answer one another. The historicity of the mission of the Twelve (Mark 6: 7-13) has often been assailed[52] on the ground that the mission belongs to the time after the resurrection; within the gospel story it is an anachronism. But the fact is that the Twelve as a group did not engage in missions after the resurrection. For the most part, so far as we can judge, they were content to stay in Jerusalem. Peter (according to Acts[53] and according to Paul[54] too) is a notable exception; there may have been others; but we can be confident that there was no general mission

31

of the Twelve. The statement of Acts 8: 1, that in the general dispersion from Jerusalem the apostles were excepted, may well be a literary device on Luke's part,[55] but Luke could hardly have used it if it had been known that the Twelve were scattered with the rest and travelled widely; and if they were bidden, as, for example, Matt. 28: 19 records, to make disciples of all the Gentiles, they were noticeably and obstinately disobedient. The question of the Gentile mission will be raised again;[56] for the moment it suffices to point out that it was not the Twelve who initiated it. Thus there was no post-resurrection mission of the Twelve to read back into the earlier story, and there is therefore a fair measure of probability that Jesus did send them out during his ministry.

This conclusion must be qualified in two ways: (a) It is likely that the charge to the messengers was to some extent written up in terms of later missionary practice. This can be seen in the complex edited charge provided by Matthew (10: 5–42), which, as study of the passage in a synopsis of the gospels will immediately show, Matthew has produced from a number of sources, and from a comparison of the Marcan charge (Mark 6: 7–11) and the Q form of the charge, which Luke appears to give in something like its original form (Luke 10: 2–16). Sets of instructions to missionaries were collected; and they were put together for use in the gospels. (b) The argument I have used points to the conclusion that Jesus may well have sent out messengers; it cannot in itself demonstrate that he called his disciples, or any of them, sheluḥin, or that on one particular occasion he sent out twelve disciples in six pairs.[57] Mark indeed does not say that he did so (though it may well be that this is what Mark himself thought). According to Mark, Jesus summoned the Twelve (who therefore, one must conclude, were not permanently at his side), and began to send them out two by two (Mark 6: 7). This could mean[58] that at some point Jesus initiated a practice of sending disciples out in pairs; and there is no reason why this should not be true. We have at least two good hints; for Mark himself (11: 1; 14: 13) records two occasions when pairs of disciples were sent on practical errands by Jesus; there may have been many such occasions; and if, as we may reasonably suppose, the disciples were themselves convinced by Jesus' proclamation of the kingdom, it would, to say the least, be surprising if they never used an opportunity of repeating it. Such trivial and incidental 'missions' would probably not be confined to the Twelve – Luke's account of the 'mission of the seventy' hints as much – and could not possibly be recorded in detail; instead, various instructions which had gained currency as the church's mission prospered were put together and attached to one simultaneous mission in which all the Twelve were sent out at once. This would be intelligible simply as a literary device, but its strongest motivation lay in the fact that it provided a picture of the Twelve that matched the way in which the Twelve were thought of at the time the gospels were written; that is, when they had been interpreted in terms of the missionary apostle Paul. (see pp. 75f).

Thus the Twelve are represented in the gospels as already incipient missionaries. It is an analogous fact that there are in the gospels passages where the Twelve are instructed to carry out a mission in the Gentile world (Matt. 28: 19; Mark 16: 15; Luke 24: 47); these, however, are among the latest parts of the tradition,[59] and the proper place to discuss them will appear later. That the Twelve as a group never did engage in such a mission is clear from Acts (whose author would gladly have recorded such a mission had he been able to do so), and from the division of labour recognized and arranged in Gal. 2: 7ff.; Peter's vocation was to the Jews. This statement, though emphatically made by Paul, needs some qualification in the light of Peter's appearance certainly at Antioch (Gal. 2: 11), and probably at Corinth[60] and at Rome,[61] and of the fact that the hand of Jerusalem was evidently felt in the Pauline churches; this, however, was anything but a mission – at most, a counter-mission, designed to put right the supposed errors and omissions in Paul's law-free preaching.

These facts lead directly to the greatest difficulty in answering the question, Who were the apostles?, namely, What are we to do with Paul? It is not wrong to reduce this question to its simplest terms. There were twelve apostles: this is stated or implied in the gospels as they stand, and in Acts, and it is repeated in a new form in Rev. 21: 14: the wall of the heavenly city has twelve foundations, and on them are the twelve names of the twelve apostles of the Lamb.[62] But the names add up to twelve without Paul, who makes no appearance in the gospel story, so that if Paul was an apostle there were not twelve apostles but (at least) thirteen. This observation is underlined by the fact that no attempt is made, natural as it would have been, to move Paul into the place vacated by Judas. If there were twelve apostles, who and what was Paul? What were such men as Barnabas, Silas, Andronicus, and Junias? Does the New Testament recognize two kinds of apostle, the Twelve and others? More important than the question, Who were the apostles? – at least if this is only a matter of listing their names – is the question, What was an apostle? how is he to be defined and recognized? by belonging to a clearly constituted group, the Twelve? by other characteristics? or by none?

The material we have so far collected about the Twelve will give us little help in answering this question, for though these disciples may have been employed by Jesus in various minor missions of a temporary kind they were apostles only in the eyes of a later generation, which used the term as a means of expressing the unique role and importance of these primary eye-witnesses of the career of Jesus of Nazareth. We must begin to answer the question from Paul, not from those who were apostles before him (Gal. 1: 17; these are not necessarily to be identified with the Twelve).[63] Apart from the fact that Paul is in any case the centre of theological thinking in the New Testament, it is right to begin with him for these reasons: (a) We have his own words. There is also in Acts a detailed narrative account of part of his apostolic ministry, but incomparably more important is the material that comes from his own hand. No other Christian writer has left us an account of what it meant to him to be an apostle. (b) Paul was deeply, thoughtfully, and passionately convinced of his call to be an apostle. In Romans, 1 and 2 Corinthians, Galatians, and Colossians he introduces himself as an apostle.[64] He lacks recognition, sometimes where he would most have valued it, but he never wavers in his own claim to apostolic status. (c) If Paul was certain of his apostleship there were others who denied it. This meant that Paul had to argue, and as other doctrines of his were hammered out in the heat of controversy so also was this. Paul's conviction that he was an apostle of Christ Jesus was tested by the scepticism of his rivals and the indifference of his converts; this obliged him to work out what his apostleship meant, and on what grounds it rested.

This means that we shall approach Paul's own view of apostleship best by reviewing some of the controversies in which he was engaged. There were self-styled apostles, pseudo-apostles, of whom Paul did not approve at all:[65]

False apostles, evil workers, making themselves look like apostles of Christ. And no marvel, for Satan himself makes himself look like an angel of light. It is no great thing therefore if his servants also make themselves look like servants of righteousness. They will get what they deserve (2 Cor. 11: 13ff.).

It is worth noting that these words imply the existence of a recognizable category of 'apostles of Christ' of which there must be genuine representatives, as well as those who are in truth servants of Satan and bogus apostles. These, we may suppose, are the intruders who have deceived and corrupted the Corinthians by preaching 'another Jesus' and a 'different Gospel', who have impressed the too impressionable members of the church by their violent and abusive – and in fact totally unapostolic – behaviour (2 Cor. 11: 2ff., 20). To be distinguished, though perhaps not entirely separated, from these false apostles are apostles of whom Paul speaks with irony – 'super-apostles', 'top apostles' (ὑπερλίαν ἀπόστολοι, 2 Cor. 11:5; 12:11). Paul never alleges that these men are servants of Satan, and deceivers (except in so far as they may deceive themselves about their own importance); but each time he refers to them he insists that he is in no way their inferior; whatever their apostolic status may be, he shares it.

These allusions in 2 Corinthians are notoriously obscure,[66] and we may ask if there is any other passage that sheds light on them. The answer is that precisely the same distinction (and association) between men who as Christian preachers were merely counterfeit and merited Paul's bitterest language, and those of whom he speaks with nothing more severe than irony, is to be found in Gal. 2. Here we encounter the 'men of name' (2:6),[67] the 'men with a name as pillars' (2:9).[68] Paul is ready to consult them, anxious indeed to do so in the interests of the mission (2:2), at the proper time. But he is not in the least impressed by them ('whatever they were makes no difference to me', 2:6); they had nothing to teach him ('they contributed nothing to me', 2:6); and he is confident that he stands on the same level as their leader, for God who created Peter's apostolate created Paul's too (2:8), so that the mission to the Gentiles is as much a part of God's purpose as the mission to the Jews. These 'men of name' are not to be distinguished from the 'super-apostles' of 2 Corinthians, to whom Paul was (he insists) no whit inferior. Galatians knows also 'false brothers',[69] who worm their way in as spies (2:4), and seek to get Gentile Christians circumcised.[70] To these men Paul yielded not even for a moment; and when, at Antioch,

Peter was infected with their opinions and changed his earlier attitude Paul did not hesitate to rebuke him.

The men who 'had a name as pillars' were James, Cephas, and John (Gal. 2:9). Two of these, Cephas and John, belonged to the inmost group of disciples which we meet in the gospels (for example, Mark 5:37). Of the original triumvirate, John's brother, James the son of Zebedee, had by this time (according to Acts 12:2) perished under Herod's sword, and his place had been taken by James the Lord's brother.[71] James's name, and his family connection, may have aided his advance, but he had seen the Lord after his resurrection (1 Cor. 15:7), and his later career, so far as we know it, suggests a character that must in any case have come to the front. Paul thus attests the existence at Jerusalem of an inner group of three, popularly known as 'pillars', probably also known as apostles, perhaps as 'super-apostles'. There were other apostles in Jerusalem: Gal. 1:17 ('I did not go up to Jerusalem to those who were apostles before me') and 1:19 ('Of the other apostles I saw none, except[72] James the Lord's brother') clearly imply this. Is this group to be identified with the Twelve? The answer to this turns to a great extent on the interpretation of 1 Cor. 15:5ff. ('he appeared to Cephas, then to the Twelve; then he appeared to more than five hundred brothers at once, of whom the majority remain to this day, but some have fallen asleep; then he appeared to James, then to all the apostles'); but the interpretation of these verses is difficult and disputed, and complicated by the fact that Paul is here citing traditional material, and possibly is combining more traditions than one. Are 'the Twelve' and 'all the apostles' to be identified? To suppose that they are to be identified not only introduces repetition coupled with a pointless change in nomenclature – if Paul is combining traditions this would be understandable – but also makes 'all' unintelligible. We know that Paul himself did not confine the apostolic office to the Twelve – if he had done so he could not have included himself[73] – and though it is conceivable that he misunderstood his sources it seems very probable that when he wrote 1 Cor. 15 he distinguished between the Twelve and all the apostles. It seems likely (judging, for the moment, simply from the Pauline evidence) that we should distinguish in Jerusalem at the time of Paul's conversion (*a*) the three reputed to be pillars; (*b*) the Twelve; (*c*) a group of apostles (who perhaps would not reside continuously in the city). The Twelve, as we have seen, were not itinerant, and most of them appear to have been men of no great significance and influence. The probability therefore is – and it is confirmed by the evidence of Gal. 2 – that in course of time the Twelve tended to drop out of the picture, leaving the direction of affairs in Jerusalem to the three 'pillars', surrounded and aided by the 'apostles' – a group within which there may sometimes have been confusion between those who had seen and been commissioned by the risen Christ (1 Cor. 15: 7), and those who were, in a secondary though in itself quite proper sense, *sheluhin* – envoys, delegates – of the leadership of the Jerusalem church. It must be remembered that the normal sense of *shaliah* is not 'missionary', but 'agent'. Gal. 2: 12 is proof that James had his envoys who made their way at least as far as Antioch, and Acts 15: 22f. describes the brothers who conveyed the apostolic letter and apostolic decree from Jerusalem to the churches of Syria and Cilicia. Such envoys, possibly out of hand and acting *ultra vires*, are probably to be seen in those who were unsettling the Galatian churches (Gal. 1 : 7), and in the false apostles whom Paul condemns in 2 Cor. 10–13. These were false apostles because they lacked a commission from Christ himself,[74] but were, or at least were acting as, no more than envoys of apostles; they were false apostles because they were not pioneer missionaries,[75] but had infiltrated into churches founded by other men, in order to propagate their own opinions and magnify their own persons; they were false apostles, above all, because neither their message nor their behaviour was Christian. They exalted themselves at the expense of their hearers, and they preached another Jesus and a different Gospel. Yet in all this they could as successfully impersonate apostles of Christ as Satan, whose servants they truly were, can make himself look like an angel of light. Both in Galatians and in 2 Corinthians, Paul's problem in dealing with these false apostles is sharpened by the fact that they appear to some extent – Paul probably did not know to what extent – to have had the backing of the Jerusalem authorities,[76] who themselves (so it seemed to Paul) did not always know their own minds, or act consistently or in complete harmony – for it is doubtful whether Peter thought and acted in precisely the same way as James.

If I were attempting here to present a history of the primitive church it would be necessary to trace these false apostles, and the 'super-apostles' whose authority they appear to have claimed, in detail. They can in fact be left in a decent and, I hope, edifying obscurity, because my only purpose in mentioning them is to bring out more clearly Paul's own conception of apostleship. I shall, however, return[77] to these various apostolic and pseudapostolic groups when I attempt to sum up the historical development of apostolic activity and terminology.

No man was more firmly convinced than Paul that he was an apostle of Christ Jesus by the will of God; this, however, was a proposition he could assert but never prove. His rivals and opponents carried with them, and collected as they went, commendatory letters[78] which vouched for their status and buttressed their authority. Paul had no such letters (2 Cor. 3: 1: 'Do we need, as some do, commendatory letters, to you, or from you?'); he could point only to people as his commendation (3: 2: 'you are our letter'), the people who as his own converts formed his own churches (1 Cor. 9: 2: 'you are the seal of my apostleship in the Lord'); and sometimes they were unwilling to act (2 Cor. 12: 11: 'I ought to have been commended by you'). They could not, however, even when they wished to do so, abdicate their position as the seal of his apostleship; they did not bestow apostleship upon him, but their existence as Christians confirmed and demonstrated it. True, he had authority, but it was authority (2 Cor. 10: 8; 13: 10) for building up (that is, for converting, and uniting converts in churches), not for throwing down (the destruction of churches by the aggressive kind of authority his rivals wielded); when disciplinary measures became necessary Paul was careful to associate the church members with himself. 1 Cor. 5: 1–5, which deals with the immoral person at Corinth, is anything but the exercise of personal authority that

41

it is often taken to be; in 2 Cor. 2: 6, punishment has been inflicted not by Paul but by the majority of the church; now he *asks* (παρακαλῶ) them to exercise love towards the offender.[79] The signs of an apostle[80] had been wrought in his churches; he could even appeal to visions and revelations, all the apparatus of *Schwär-merei*, 'enthusiasm' in the bad sense, but he knew as he did so that he acted like a fool (2 Cor. 12: 1, 11). He rejected the privilege of living, and supporting a wife, at the expense of the church, preferring rather to work for his keep (1 Cor. 9: 1–18; 2 Cor. 11: 7–11; 12: 13), and to employ what time and energy were left him in the service of the Gospel and the care of the churches. He was one of the apostolic company that stood forth under the scorn of men and angels, under sentence of death, the scum of the earth, nobodies, unknown, unable to prove that Christ spoke in them and therefore judged to be deceivers, flogged, stoned, shipwrecked, burning with shame and humiliation (for example, 1 Cor. 4: 9–13; 2 Cor. 4: 7–12; 6: 4–10; 11: 23–33).

All this, and yet not only treating with love and courtesy those who treated him with contumely and scorn, but aware that he personally occupied a signifi-cant place in the final working out of God's plan for mankind – for Fridrichsen[81] was right when he said that Paul, as one 'called to be an apostle' claimed to be an 'eschatologic person', one, that is, who had his own place in God's timetable for the last days, and would play his own part in bringing about the consum-mation. Paul's work, as apostle of the Gentiles, would issue in the salvation not of the Gentiles only, but of Israel too;[82] he could in his own person help to fill up the tale of messianic affliction[83] that must be endured before the arrival of the Age to Come (Col. 1: 24). This he could be and do because he had been drawn into the eschatological events of the crucifixion and resurrection of Jesus. The risen Lord he had himself seen: as latest and least (1 Cor. 15: 8), he had been drawn into this historical manifestation of the non-historical, of the power and majesty of God. But the risen Lord was the Lord who had been crucified, and it was the Paul who had been crucified with Christ who now lived by faith in the Son of God who loved him and had given himself for him (Gal. 2: 19ff.). He writes (2 Cor. 4: 10f.):

We always carry round the dying (νέϰρωσιν) of Jesus in our body, that the life of Jesus too may be manifested in our body. For we living men are always being handed over to death for Jesus' sake, that the life of Jesus too may be manifested in our mortal flesh.

But Paul concludes (4: 12):

So then death is at work in us, but life in you.

The apostolic mission plunges Paul into the heart of the messianic affliction, without which there is no victory for the people of God, and this determines the spectacle that the apostle, the microcosm of the church, presents to the world.

We are weak in him, but we shall live with him by the power of God (2 Cor. 13: 4).

Paul's theology bears the stamp of the Cross, and so does his apostolic ministry; it bears the imprint of the resurrection too, but just as the crucifixion of Jesus was a public event, known to all men, reported even by the secular historian Tacitus,[84] whereas the

43

resurrection was known to few (cf. John 14: 22; Acts 10: 41), and to them by direct divine disclosure (not, as far as Paul is concerned, by inference from an empty tomb), so what is generally visible in Paul's apostleship is the sign of the Cross.

Thus he becomes, as an apostle, a fool for Christ's sake (1 Cor. 4: 10), the same sort of fool that Christ himself had been, when he bore the burden of sins that were not his own, and refused to prove the truth of his own case by coming down from the cross, choosing rather to die deserted, misunderstood, and in despair, than to betray those whose cause he had taken up, to deny the truth, and to play false to God – even when God appeared to abandon him. Hence in turn the pioneering evangelistic drive of Paul, who, because he was under obligation to Greeks and barbarians, wise and foolish (Rom. 1: 14), would never build on another man's foundation but was continually pressing on, that Christ's name might be heard where it had never been heard before (Rom. 15: 20; 2 Cor. 10: 12–16); hence the fact that he can do nothing against but only for the truth (2 Cor. 13: 8); hence the pastoral responsibility that lets itself be trampled on, to the glory of God.

It is hard to cram this Pauline picture into a miniature frame, and it would be well if we had time to work out the paradoxical epigram of strength made perfect in weakness (2 Cor. 12: 9) in biographical terms. In the time available this cannot be done; indeed, much has been left out of the picture as it has been sketched here, and before we leave Paul a few more of the facts about his use of the word 'apostle' must be quickly noted. He uses it in at least two senses. Epaphroditus is described as 'your [the Philippians'] apostle' (Phil. 2:25); that is, the man whom you sent on a specific mission, namely, to convey the present of money you were making available to meet my physical needs. Similarly the brothers of 2 Cor. 8:23 are 'apostles of churches', that is, envoys sent by various churches to carry out specific duties (in this case, financial duties connected with Paul's collection for the poor of the Jerusalem church). In these passages the word (ἀπόστολος) simply means 'envoy', 'accredited representative'; its background (since there is little in Greek that could account for it)[85] is the Jewish use of the word *shaliaḥ*. They add little (except, it may be, a measure of confusion) to a study of Paul's conception of apostleship. At the other end of the scale is Paul's full use of the word 'apostle', pre-eminently in passages in which he applies it to himself. In addition to what has already been said about Paul's understanding of what it meant to be an apostle, the following points may be noted here:

(a) Paul uses the word with two genitives. The first is the personal name, 'Christ Jesus'.[86] Is the genitive subjective ('one who has been sent by Christ Jesus'), or possessive ('an envoy who is the property of Christ Jesus')? It is probably right to reject the alternative and to answer, Both.[87] If the word 'apostle' means, as it does, 'a person who has been sent', no one can have done the sending (in Paul's view) but Christ Jesus. But again, Christ Jesus sent Paul not to do anything that he pleased but to act as his (Christ's) slave,[88] so that as an apostle Paul was equally the slave, the property, of Christ Jesus. It is fair to say that the genitive 'of Christ Jesus' implies both a specific commission (which Paul probably connected with the appearance to him of the risen Christ – 1 Cor. 15: 8; Gal. 1: 16) and a permanent obligation to unquestioning service at any cost. The second genitive is 'of the Gentiles'.[89] This represents the direction of Paul's mission: he is an apostle with a special commission to preach to and convert Gentiles; cf. Gal. 2: 7.[90] This conviction, and the arrangement made with the Jerusalem authorities, did not mean that Paul ceased to feel responsibility for the Jews; apart from the fact that he continued to preach to Jews as well as to Gentiles, and to experience their reaction to his message (1 Cor. 1: 23f.), he believed that his Gentile mission would promote the salvation of Israel.[91]

(b) Though Paul conceived his apostleship in an individual way, he did not suppose that he was the only apostle. When he claims (2 Cor. 11: 5; 12: 11) that he is not excelled by the 'super-apostles' he implicitly allows that their status is at least comparable with his. 1 Cor. 9: 5 with its reference to 'the *other* apostles' bears the same implication.

Does Paul use the word 'apostle' in a third sense, to denote a body of men who were more than church messengers[92] but less than apostles such as himself and Peter? What were Andronicus and Junias?[93] Passages that might suggest a second-grade apostleship are (in addition to Rom. 16: 7) 1 Cor. 15: 7 (if these 'apostles' are to be distinguished from the Twelve, and full apostleship is restricted to the latter), 2 Cor. 11: 13 (if this means that the false apostles both recognized their subordination to the 'super-apostles' and claimed to be apostles), and conceivably 1 Cor. 12: 28 (if the apostles here are, like the prophets, teachers and so forth, to be thought of as local Christian leaders). It can hardly be claimed that any of these passages is convincing; and against them is to be set 1 Thess. 2: 7, where Paul appears to group Silvanus and Timothy with himself as apostles.[94] When the whole Pauline evidence is reviewed, it is much easier to establish the two extremes – apostles of Christ Jesus, such as Paul himself and Peter, and envoys of churches – than to pick out a clearly defined intermediate category. Such categorization belonged to a later period than Paul's.

This observation may provide the cue for us to leave Paul and turn to other parts of the New Testament; and first, to Acts. It is here that the problem of the number of the apostles becomes most acute. The early chapters assume that there is a limited group of apostles, and that there are twelve of them. Acts 1: 2, summing up the appearances of the risen Jesus and reconstituting the apostolic group, with its reference to the 'apostles whom he had chosen (ἐξελέξατο)', points clearly to Luke 6: 13, 'out of [his disciples] he chose (ἐκλεξάμενος) twelve' – the twelve[95] are the witnesses of the resurrection and thus the link between Jesus and the church as it begins and continues its own existence in history. That these persons are those concerned, or at least primarily concerned, in the next events, the promises and commission of Jesus (1: 7f.) and his ascension (1: 9ff.), is confirmed by the list of eleven names in 1: 13, and by the differentiation of this group from (and its association with) the women, Mary the mother of Jesus, and his brothers in 1: 14. On the day of Pentecost Peter stood up with the eleven[96] (2: 14), and the same group is in mind in 2: 37 (Peter and the other apostles). 'The apostles' are mentioned at 4: 33ff. (cf. 36f.) without reference to a number, but it is scarcely doubtful that Luke had the usual limited group in mind.[97] Acts 5: 2, 12 invite the same comment, and so does the rest of chapter 5, where 'the apostles' are brought before the Jewish Council, especially in view of 6: 2, which again, and for the last time in Acts, gives the number of the apostles as twelve. It is scarcely necessary to pursue the rest of the material in detail: 8: 1, 14, 18; 9: 27; 11: 1; 15: 2, 4, 6, 22, 23; 16: 4 all represent the apostles as a closed group, set over against sometimes 'the brothers' (11: 1), sometimes 'the elders' (15: 2, 4, 6, 22, 23; 16: 4).

The most important passages are chapters 1 and 6. In 1: 15–26 Matthias is elected to fill the place left vacant by the defection of Judas.[98] Nothing could underline more heavily the significance of the number twelve.[99] It is not that twelve men, no less, are needed to do the work, for no attempt is made to fill the place of the martyred James (Acts 12: 2). Death removes James from the work, but not from the number; evidently what matters is that the number twelve be kept intact. Rengstorf, after showing that the election of Matthias displays a continuing concern for the mission to Israel, adds a second reason for Luke's interest in it:[100]

If, so soon after Pentecost, Luke lets the Twelve as a whole disappear from the stage, he wants to make known that after the outpouring of the Holy Spirit questions of organization are of secondary importance for the church, because through the Holy Spirit the risen Lord himself leads and governs his church.

There is substance in this view, and we shall return to it,[101] but it needs some qualification in view of the fact

that in 6: 2[102] Luke still distinguishes the Twelve by
number from the rest of the church, and not only from
the rest of the church at large but specifically from the
Seven. It is, notwithstanding 6: 1, quite clear that the
Seven became anything but mere catering officers, and
most students of Acts would agree that more lies behind
their position in the early church than the needs of the
Hellenist widows; they were the leaders of a divergent,
or at least of a distinct, wing of the church.[103] From
the standpoint of Luke's generation it must have
seemed a simple and natural expedient to assimilate
them to the Twelve; this, however, Luke does not do,
but rather marks the Seven off from the Twelve with
unmistakable clarity, introducing a distinct subordination in the process.

There were, then, twelve apostles. Inevitably this
raises the question, What of Paul? He was no subordinate figure; rather, if Acts has a human hero, it is he.
It has often been pointed out that he at least balances
Peter in importance, and it is sometimes claimed that
Luke deliberately wrote parallel narratives, that the
one might not outshine the other. Concerning this, it
is well, with Harnack (and many others), to be cautious:
'This, however, does not admit of proof'.[104] In the end,
Paul supersedes Peter, for after 15: 14 Peter drops out
and Paul is left in undisputed possession of the centre
of the stage; or, if his position is rivalled, it is rivalled
by the other great non-member of the Twelve, James
(Acts 21: 18). Outstanding, however, as the figure of
Paul in Acts is, since there are twelve apostles and no
more, Acts can hardly call him 'the apostle Paul' and
does not do so, though on occasion the unofficial use of
'apostle' as 'missionary' slips through (Acts 14: 4, 14),

applied equally to Paul and Barnabas. In the apostolic letter these two seem to be distinguished from the apostles who write it (15: 25f.: 'we decided at our assembly to choose men to send to you together with our dear Barnabas and Saul, men who have devoted their lives for the name of our Lord Jesus Christ'), though they are cordially associated with them. This differs so radically from the material in the epistles that it becomes necessary to look with a critical eye at Luke's conception of apostleship.

The 'Paulinism' of Acts has of late been severely handled[105] – perhaps too severely, for the contents of the book prove clearly enough, as we have seen, that the author was at least some kind of Paulinist,[106] whose worst crime (and it is one that most of us share) was perhaps that of being a less profound and perceptive theologian than his hero, and of living in a different age. This is a pardonable offence; I should not, however, wish to suggest that it is a trivial matter, or to defend Luke in some of the ways in which he has been defended. According to Wilckens[107] Luke appears as the corrupter of the Pauline Gospel only if we have already interpreted Paul existentially. 'But the existentially interpreted Paul is not the historical Paul.' I am not so sure: to walk by faith, not by sight (2 Cor. 5: 7) is not very different from 'the perpetually new decision of the individual'.[108] There is more substance in Flender's contention[109] that just as Paul, in faithfulness, not unfaithfulness, to Jesus, had in a new generation to say things that Jesus had not said, so Luke, in a third generation, had, in faithfulness to Paul, to say things Paul had not said. This needs to be qualified by the observation that between the time of Jesus and the time of Paul stood the great positive event of the crucifixion and resurrection, whereas that which separated the time of Paul from that of Luke was simply the extension of time, which carried with it only the negative event of the non-arrival of the *parousia*. It is true that Luke fails to penetrate the depths of sin and the riches of salvation that Paul sees exposed in the Cross; true too, and an inevitable consequence of this, that he does not see the problem of the Gentile mission as Paul did. For Paul, the mission rested on the discovery that Jew and Gentile alike were all under sin (Rom. 3: 9, 23) and that Christ was the end of the law (Rom. 10: 4), with the consequent disintegration of Jewish religious life[110] and the dissolution of all distinction (Rom. 3: 22; 10: 12); for Luke it was something nearer to a recognition that Gentiles at their best could be just as good as Jews (for example, Acts 10: 34f.), that God accepted them as such, and that it would therefore be a pity to exclude them. This theological difference, even if it can be thinned down to a difference in emphasis (and I am doubtful whether it can), resulted in a different historical picture, for Acts shows little trace of the problems of the Gentile mission, and of the controversies between Paul and Jerusalem, that reverberate through the epistles. Who, reading the friendly discussion between James, Peter, and Paul in Acts 15, would suspect that the first had excommunicated the third and his followers (Gal. 2: 12f.), or suppose that Paul could accuse the majority of his fellow-preachers of adulterating the word of God (2 Cor. 2: 17)?[111] It was not part of Luke's purpose of edifying and instructing the church in his own day to dig out these disreputable (but fundamental and highly significant) conflicts. It is not that he was dishonest; probably he did not see, as we should be able to see, the value of these conflicts for the church of every subsequent age; probably, because of his theological presuppositions, he was simply unable to get a clear view of what happened, even when his sources might have permitted this.

If these observations are correct, we shall not be surprised if Acts reveals a different conception of apostleship from Paul's. And so in fact it does. Historically, Luke's anxiety to represent the church in its mission to the world as the outcome of, and as continuous with, Jesus and his mission to Israel, leads him to tie down the notion of apostleship to the group of twelve whom he could describe as having been close disciples and companions of Jesus during his ministry,[112] and to represent these twelve as responsible, through Peter, for initiating the Gentile mission (Acts 10: 1–48), and collectively sanctioning and controlling it (8: 14–17; 11: 1–18, 22; 15: 22–29).[113] This means that no room is left for conflict; as we have seen, the reader of Acts will search in vain for any of the stresses that 'caused the writing of that long-drawn-out, harassed groan, which is the Second Epistle to the Corinthians'.[114] Hence, with but few exceptions, apostles pursue their way in peace, favoured by the authorities (for example, 13: 12; 19: 37), released from prison by earthquake or angelic intervention (5: 19; 12: 7; 16: 26), almost uniformly successful, and seriously resisted only by the Jews, who had already manifested their malignity in their opposition to Jesus. In this success story the paradox and profundity of Pauline apostleship disappear. Not quite; for I have not been fair to Acts. Apostles do rejoice that they are counted worthy to suffer for the sake of the Name (5: 41); Peter is three times thrown into prison, and stands on the verge of execution (4: 3; 5: 18; 12: 3); Paul is called to suffer (9: 16; cf. 22: 18; 26: 16f.), and does suffer – stoning (14: 19), imprisonment (16: 23; 22: 24), mobbing (22: 22), shipwreck (27: 40–44) – and warns his converts that it is through suffering that they will enter the kingdom of God. But these things are kept in their place, and the general impression is that which I have described. It is in the first instance a narrative impression, but it has theological implications, and to some extent arises out of theological and ecclesiastical presuppositions. The apostle tends to become a figurehead, and so to point towards a theology of glory; that is, he becomes a leader in the forward movement of the church, as its Gospel spreads outward from Jerusalem to the ends of the earth (Acts 1: 8); he, and humbler Christians with him, are inspired by the Spirit, and never really perplexed as to their true course (8: 26, 29; 10: 19; 16: 6f.); new developments in the church and its mission that do not spring directly from his own initiative require his confirmation (8: 14); he constitutes in his own person a link with Jesus, the founder of the new faith, and (in consultation with the church as a whole, and especially with its elders) lays down the law for its behaviour. This development in Acts corresponds with the frequently observed lack of emphasis in Luke on the suffering and death of Jesus. Even so, however, the point made above on p. 48 must be borne in mind. Luke is not greatly interested in the organization of the church, or in its developing sacramentalism; he may present us with some of the raw material of 'primitive catholicism', but hardly with the thing itself.

Other parts of the New Testament can receive only scanty treatment, but some attempt must be made to collect and review the remainder of the evidence. We may begin from the Pastoral Epistles, since these are closely related to Acts.[115] In them, as in Acts, Paul is beyond question the 'hero', the apostle *par excellence*. No other, indeed, is named or even alluded to. Paul writes as an apostle (1 Tim. 1: 1; 2 Tim. 1: 1; Tit. 1: 1), and the major purposes of the epistles are at the same time to vindicate him, and to cause his voice to be heard in a later age.[116] Though the epistles as a whole cannot be regarded as Paul's own work, the understanding of the apostle that they contain is not so far from that of the historical Paul himself as is sometimes supposed. Two verses, 1 Tim. 2: 7 and 2 Tim. 1: 11, depict the apostle in terms that he himself would have recognized, though they are not terms that he used: as an apostle he is a herald (κῆρυξ), and a teacher of the Gentiles. It may be true[117] that Paul deliberately avoided the term 'herald' because the herald was a sacrosanct person, who might not be harmed even by the enemies of his people, and he, Paul, knew that an apostle was not the most protected but the most vulnerable and exposed of men; if this is true, the author of the Pastorals was less sensitive than Paul to a subtlety of linguistic usage, but he cannot be accused of treating the apostle as a guarded, sacrosanct figure.

In which [the Gospel] I suffer even bonds, as if I were a criminal; but the word of God is not bound. For this reason I endure all things for the sake of the elect, that they too may attain salvation in Christ Jesus, with eternal glory (2 Tim. 2: 9f.).

This is precisely Paul's own attitude: he must suffer, but the Gospel is free.

Other passages (for example, 2 Tim. 3: 10f.) list the sufferings of the apostle, and whether or not 2 Tim. 4 contains passages from a genuine letter written on the eve of Paul's execution,[118] this is the setting that the author has provided for the epistle. It is true that, though of course he cannot deny or conceal Paul's death, he does his best to provide the story with a happy ending, and inevitably there is nothing to match the dramatic – and theological – power of 1 Cor. 4: 9–13; 2 Cor. 4: 7–10; 6: 4–10; 11: 23–33; yet the Paul of the Pastorals knows himself to be the chief of sinners (1 Tim. 1: 15[119]), to be under the necessity of dying with Christ (2 Tim. 2: 11), and to be the preacher of the grace and mercy of God (1 Tim. 1: 11–16). It is this preaching that the author desires to safeguard (most clearly in 2 Tim. 2: 2), and the historical Paul was concerned to safeguard it too (for example, Gal. 1: 8f.). It is primarily the lapse of time that puts the process of safeguarding in a somewhat different perspective, and makes the Paul of the Pastorals represent himself as the author of a tradition that must be handed down intact from one generation to the next. Even this, however, does not do justice to the Pastorals, for the true doctrine, the deposit ($\pi\alpha\varrho\alpha\theta\acute{\eta}\varkappa\eta$) of faith, is the responsibility of the Holy Spirit (2 Tim. 1: 14), and it is God himself who in the last resort will guard it (2 Tim. 1: 12). This means that it is only in at most a subsidiary sense that the apostle is regarded as the fountain-head of tradition, and in this respect the Pastorals differ markedly from later Christian literature.

It is a striking fact that the Pastorals, differing sharply in this from Acts, make no reference to apostles other than Paul. The Twelve completely disappear. This can hardly be thought fortuitous in documents that set out to establish the basis of church and ministry. It need not mean, and probably does not mean, that the author intended by his silence to attack the apostolic status of the Twelve; by the end of the first century this was too firmly established to be attacked by anything less whole-hearted than Marcion's[120] total revaluation of Christian origins. It cannot, however, mean less than that he took Paul as the standard of apostleship, and was concerned that the Pauline understanding of apostleship (as he himself had understood it) should prevail, and provide the pattern for the church's ministry. As we shall see,[121] the leading apostles, who already in Gal. 2 show signs of becoming ecclesiastical bureaucrats, tended to be thought of as ecclesiastical dictators, and the picture of the Twelve drawn in Acts had the effect of encouraging this tendency; the Pastorals, so far from furthering it, by their silence and by their emphasis on the solitary figure of the wandering and persecuted Paul, combated it, and sought to write the Pauline doctrine of apostleship into the structure of the church.[122]

In some respects the Epistle to the Ephesians resembles the Pastorals: Paul is the great apostle, especially the man entrusted by God with responsibility for the Gentiles (3: 1, 6, 8). But Ephesians also knows 'the apostles' as a group who, with the prophets,[123] form the foundation of the church (2: 20). This foundation they are in virtue of the disclosure to them of the divine mystery of salvation in Christ (3: 5),[124] and particularly of the fact (3: 6) that the Gentiles are to be included within the scope of this salvation, and thus of the people of God. Paul himself, as the paragraph goes on to show, has the special function of putting this new availability of salvation into effect, but he does this as the representative agent of the whole company of apostles and prophets. This is much nearer than the Pastorals to the picture painted in Acts, where, as we have seen, Peter, the representative of the Twelve, is made the first preacher to the Gentiles and the defender of the Gentile mission, though he is subsequently replaced in these functions by Paul. In another form, and one more comprehensive than the Pastorals, Ephesians represents the victory of the Pauline view of apostleship, in that Paul becomes the leader and outstanding representative of the whole apostolic group, who can no longer be thought of as a company of twelve excluding Paul. The victory, however, is a dangerous one, for Paul, in being accepted with the Twelve, is in some danger of being taken over by those whom he is depicted as representing. Eph. 4: 11, which appears to be based on 1 Cor. 12: 28, suggests the survival of an older terminology, and perhaps of older ways and institutions. Here there is nothing to suggest that apostles and prophets form the same kind of closed group that they were in 2: 20; 3: 5; and we should probably think of the missionaries of the earlier period.[125]

Of 1 Peter all that can be said here is that it too, in a different way, represents a victory of the Pauline understanding of apostleship, for Peter is made to appear as a second Paul, a pastor of churches spread through the Gentile world (1 Peter 1:1f.), exercising his pastoral responsibility no longer in person but by letter, as Paul had done, bearing witness to the true grace of God as the foundation of Christian life, and exhorting his readers to appropriate behaviour (5:12 – an excellent summary of the epistle). To say this is not to deny that the historical Peter may have exercised pastoral care over a number of churches; it is probable that he travelled widely, and if he did so he must have assumed pastoral responsibilities. But as the form of the letter is that of the Pauline letters, so is the form of apostleship which the writer adopts that of the Pauline model.[126]

In this short sketch nothing need be said of the Epistle of James, and of Hebrews only that this epistle is unique in reserving the title 'apostle' for Jesus himself (Heb. 3:1), and refers to the primary guarantors of Christian truth in general terms (the salvation spoken by the Lord 'was confirmed to us by those who heard him'; 2:3).

Jude and 2 Peter represent the form in which orthodox Christian belief about the apostles settled down in the second century, and really belong, in this respect at least, to the development after the New Testament rather than to the New Testament itself. This appears in its earliest and simplest form in Jude 17: Christians of Jude's time must remember the words spoken previously ($\pi\rho\sigma\varepsilon\iota\rho\eta\mu\acute{\varepsilon}\nu\omega\nu$) by the 'apostles of our Lord Jesus Christ'. They foretold the appearance of impious mockers; these men have now arisen and Christians, being forewarned, should be forearmed against them. 2 Peter 3:2 takes up and elaborates the same point: 'the things spoken previously by the holy prophets, and the commandment of the Lord and Saviour delivered to you[127] by your apostles'. In doing this, the author for the moment forgets that he is writing in the name of one of these apostles: 'Symeon Peter, slave and apostle of Jesus Christ' (1: 1). He is, however, making the same point in the reference to apostles in 3: 2 as in his use of pseudonymity, for Peter is introduced in order to serve as a surety for the purity of the Christian faith as it has been handed down from the earliest days. In particular, Peter is able to remind his readers that their faith does not rest upon artificial myths (1: 16); for example, Peter himself witnessed the Transfiguration, and is able to guarantee the truth of the record (1: 16ff.). For those who oppose this apostolic faith no words are too hard; they are corrupt alike in mind and in morals. No serious refutation, or even statement, of their position is brought forward; Symeon Peter's only argument is vituperation, with a firm repetition of orthodox formulas.

The apostolic church has one problem, created not by pressure from without but by embarrassment and possible betrayal from within; it is caused by 'our dear brother Paul' (3: 15), whose epistles have proved too useful for the heretics. Of course, this is only because the heretics pervert them (3: 16); brother Paul did not in fact mean anything other than the rest of his apostolic brethren, and his writings are not for private but only for authorized interpretation (1: 20, with 3: 16: 'the other scriptures'). Thus understood and safeguarded, Paul may be brought within the apostolic college and receive Peter's *imprimatur*, and the Pauline problem, which had vexed the church of the first century and certainly continued to exist, though in new forms, in

59

the second century,[128] may be conveniently settled by the domestication of Paul. This epistle is more important as a witness to the problem than as a solution to it.[129] Whether the Jerusalem authorities, for whom 'the Twelve' became a symbol,[130] believed their position to be irreconcilable with Paul's can now perhaps never be determined. But the conception of apostleship they came to stand for (whether or not they themselves historically had stood for it) could never be at peace with a free Paul. It is at this point that a study of apostleship leads into the heart of the problems both of New Testament history and of New Testament theology, and into the problems of the early church too.

There remains one large and vitally important part of the New Testament, which is more likely than any other to point to a solution of the problems I have just sketched. This is the Johannine literature. It is highly improbable that all five documents (the gospel, three epistles, and Revelation) were written by the same author, but there is sufficient unity within them for us to consider them now as a whole. They are certainly not, however, a unit in their use of the term 'apostle'. I have already noted that Rev. 21: 14 contains as clear a statement as can be found anywhere in the New Testament of the view that there are twelve apostles, neither more nor fewer: the twelve names of the twelve apostles of the Lamb are written on the twelve foundations of the city. But the word is used in two other places in different senses. Rev. 18: 20 recalls 1 Cor. 12: 28; Eph. 4: 11:

Rejoice over her, heaven, and the saints, and the apostles, and the prophets, for God has avenged you on her.

Rev. 2: 2 is different again:

Thou didst test those who say they are apostles, and are not, and didst find them false.

It is implied that there is a distinct group of persons known as apostles, which is not unlimited, so that any-one may claim, truly or falsely, to belong to it, and that his claim may be tested; it is implied too that false claims were in fact made.[131]

The word 'apostle' does not occur in the Johannine epistles, and in the gospel only once, and that without any technical meaning. It is simply a verbal noun meaning 'someone sent'.[132]

A slave is not greater than his master, nor is one who is sent (ἀπόστολος) greater than the one who sent him (τοῦ πέμψαντος αὐτόν) (John 13: 16).

We have already considered the names of disciples found in John;[133] the special designation 'the Twelve' is used on two occasions. In 20: 24 Thomas is described as 'one of the Twelve'; and in 6: 66–71 several synoptic themes connected with this group reappear. When many of his disciples withdraw, Jesus challenges the Twelve with the question, 'Do you too mean to go away?' This may be said to be equivalent to the synoptic selection and appointment of the Twelve, though as it stands it presupposes their existence as a distinct group. Peter replies that withdrawal is impossible: 'Thou hast the words of eternal life; . . . thou art the Holy One of God.' This corresponds to the confession of Peter in the synoptic tradition. Jesus comments: 'Have I not chosen you, the Twelve, and one of you is a devil?' The next verse makes explicit that it is Judas Iscariot that is in mind. That the traitor was one of the group of twelve is also a synoptic tradition. Since Thomas is in the synoptic lists it appears that throughout this material John is making use of the earlier tradition (or something very much like it).

It might thus seem that the Johannine literature has little to contribute to the theme of apostleship; but this is not so. It contributes so much that the theme cannot be seriously pursued in the space available here;[134] for between them the gospel and the epistles[135] raise in the acutest form the question what authority is to be ascribed to the eyewitnesses of the work of Jesus, and the related but distinct question how this authority, whatever it may have been, is transmitted within the life of the church. These questions are not identical with the historical questions, Who were the apostles? What did they do and teach? How did they behave?; but they are the theological questions that underlie the historical inquiry which we have up to now been pursuing.

Consider the following passages:

The word became flesh and dwelt among us, and we beheld his glory (John 1: 14).

We speak what we know, and bear witness of what we have seen (John 3: 11).

If I bear witness about myself my witness is not true; but there is another who bears witness about me, and I know that the witness he bears about me is true (John 5: 31f.).

Even if I bear witness about myself my witness is true, for I know where I have come from and where I am going (John 8: 14).

When the Paraclete comes . . . he will bear witness about me; and you also bear witness, because you have been with me from the beginning (John 15: 26f.).

As my Father has sent me, so do I send you (John 20: 21).

This is the disciple who bears witness about these things and wrote these things, and we know that his witness is true (John 21: 24).

That which was from the beginning, which we have heard, which we have seen with our eyes, which we beheld and our hands handled . . . that which we have seen and heard, we report to you also (1 John 1: 1,3).

My little children, I am writing these things to you that you may not sin. . . . By this we know that we have come to know him (1 John 2: 1,3).

I am not writing to you because you do not know the truth, but because you know it (1 John 2: 21).

Beloved, do not believe every spirit, but test the spirits to see whether they come from God, for many false prophets have gone out into the world (1 John 4: 1).

Demetrius has witness borne to him by all men, and by the truth itself; and we too bear him witness, and you know that our witness is true. I had many things to write to you, but I do not wish to write with pen and ink (3 John 12f.).

These quotations illustrate, by no means exhaustively, a subtle interplay between the pronouns 'I', 'we', and 'you'. This must not be oversimplified into the question (with reference, for example, to John 1: 14) of the authorship of the gospel: was it or was it not written by an eyewitness of the ministry of Jesus?[136] Nor is it answered if we can decide (as indeed we cannot)[137] whether the epistles (or one, or two, of them) were written by the evangelist. The question that is raised is that which will be handled, in a different context, in the second main part of this lecture: How does the church remain apostolic when there are no apostles left? The answer to this question can be given only if we can first answer the question, What makes an apostle an apostle? Or, in more Johannine form, What constitutes the original, apostolic, authoritative, determinative witness to Jesus Christ? There is no single answer to this question; or rather, the answer to it involves a number of factors, none of which can be omitted.

First stands the gracious predestinating divine choice of men to act as servants of the word – of the word incarnate, and of the word that proclaims the word incarnate.

You have not chosen me, but I have chosen you, and I appointed you that you might go and bear fruit, and that your fruit might last (John 15: 16; cf. 6: 70; 13: 18).
He who is of God hears the words of God (John 8: 47; cf. 18: 37).
As my Father has sent me, so I send you (John 20: 21; cf. 17: 18).
Feed my lambs. . . . tend my lambs. . . . feed my lambs (John 21: 15ff.).

Second: those whom God thus appoints actually behold his act in history in the person of his Son. It might suffice simply to draw attention to the existence of the gospel as a record (open as it is to critical investigation, and imperfect as a historical account); but the evidence is much more emphatic even than this.

The word became flesh, and dwelt among us, and we beheld his glory (John 1: 14).
He that has seen has borne witness (John 19: 35).
He saw and believed (John 20: 8).
That which we have heard, that which we have seen with our eyes, that which we beheld and our hands handled (1 John 1: 1).
This is how you know the Spirit of God: Every spirit that confesses that Jesus Christ has come in the flesh is of God,

and every spirit that does not so confess Jesus is not of God; and this is the spirit of Antichrist (1 John 4: 2f.).

Third: merely to 'behold' does not make an apostle or disciple. He must also hear (that is, hear, keep, and obey) the word of Jesus.

If you abide in my word, you are truly my disciples (John 8: 31).
If anyone loves me he will keep my word, . . . he who does not love me does not keep my words; and the word that you hear is not mine but the Father's that sent me (John 14: 23f.; cf. 12: 47f.).
He who says, I know him, and does not keep his commandments, is a liar, and the truth is not in him; whoever keeps his word, truly God's love has been perfected in him (1 John 2: 4f.).

Fourth: the human witness of those who thus hear and obey, and bear witness to what they have seen and heard, is supported, and indeed made possible, by the witness of the Holy Spirit.

When the Paraclete comes . . . he will bear witness about me; and you too bear witness, because you have been with me from the beginning (John 15: 26f.).
When he comes, the Spirit of truth, he will lead you into all the truth, for he will not speak of himself, but will speak what he hears, and will announce to you the events to come. He will glorify me, because he will take of what belongs to me and announce it to you (John 16: 13f.).

Immediately after the commission quoted above from John 20: 21 follows the act that makes the commission possible:

When he had said this he breathed into them and said to them, Receive the Holy Spirit (John 20: 22).

Because they have received the Spirit, disciples know the truth and have an inward conviction and testimony to it.

You have an anointing from the Holy One, and you all have knowledge (1 John 2: 20).
As for you, the anointing that you have received from him abides in you, and you have no need that anyone should teach you; but as his anointing teaches you about all things, and is true and is no lie, and as it taught you, you abide in it[138] (1 John 2: 27).
He who believes in the Son of God has the witness in him. He who does not believe God has made him a liar, because he has not believed in the testimony God bore concerning his Son (1 John 5: 10).

It will be seen that these four points depend on two things only: one is the continued operation of the Holy Spirit, which is a matter of God's faithfulness to his own word; the other is the continued existence of the apostolic testimony to Jesus Christ, the word that men may hear, trust, and obey. That the new generation has not seen the incarnate word is no defect in its apostolicity:

Because you have seen me, you have believed; blessed are those who have not seen, yet believed (John 20: 29).

The main intention of this verse is not to belittle the importance of that which, once for all, was seen, or of the apostolic faith of the first generation that rested upon this sight; it is rather to affirm that each generation of Christians may share the blessedness of those who saw with their eyes and handled with their hands. This blessedness is not dependent upon a particular group of apostles, or a theory of apostleship, or on descendants or successors of the apostles. It is dependent on the original testimony of those who saw;[139] upon the hearing and believing of the apostolic word; and upon the continuing ministry of the Holy Spirit.

It will be clear that transition to the second part of this lecture cannot now be long delayed. Before we leave the first part, two tasks remain. The historical and theological conclusions suggested by the material we have sketched must be briefly summed up. The former remain enigmatic and uncertain;[140] the latter can be stated with some confidence.

I turn first to the historical question, with the promise to avoid oversimplification except so far as this is demanded by brevity, and the reminder that a good deal of the evidence has already been outlined.

Jesus appears in the gospels as a teacher;[141] if he taught, he must have had pupils, or disciples. It is stated in the gospels, and can hardly fail to have been true, that some of these stood closer to him than others; out of the total company a smaller group was formed. Its formation was not necessarily a formal act that took place at a particular time; the gospels (for example, Mark 3: 14) describe it in this way, but it must be remembered that they were written on a very small scale, so that a measure of formalizing was necessary if all essential matters were to be mentioned. Jesus, however, was more than a teacher; he acted as well as spoke with a special authority,[142] and his closest followers were more than pupils;[143] indeed, their obedience to his authority, sadly imperfect as it was, was a more important characteristic of them than their understanding of his teaching. Here too there must have been gradation between the committed and the peripheral.

Whether the inner group of disciples was ever, on one particular occasion, sent out to conduct a preaching and healing mission within Israel must remain doubtful;[144] there can be little doubt that they were sent from time to time to perform specific tasks for their master, and these must have shaded into proclamation. If, for example, they were sent ahead to prepare a night's lodging, would they not have something to say about the person for whom they claimed this service? This group of pupils and servants[145] was no doubt to some extent fluid. This would explain the tradition of a stable core of three or four, and some marginal fluctuation in the list of names. As envoys they could easily have been described as *sh*ᵉ*luḥin*;[146] this word does not mean, or necessarily imply, 'missionaries'.

The ministry of Jesus came to an end with the crucifixion, and the resurrection saw the re-establishment of a group of his followers in Jerusalem. This could not be other than the group which had stood by him nearly till the last. There had been at least one notable defection (Judas), and one partial defection (Peter); there may have been more. But at least there was a substantial continuity between the group that had lived with Jesus, and that which constituted the nucleus of the Jerusalem church. At this time, if not before, their number was established as twelve, to correspond with the tribes who still in theory represented the totality of Israel. The number may go back to Jesus, who directed his own mission to Israel and may have seen his disciples as representing the fruit (this, perhaps, rather than the agents) of it; at least it belongs to the early days in Jerusalem, for the old tradition of 1 Cor. 15: 5 connects it with the resurrection. These Twelve were anything but missionaries to the Gentiles. There is no evidence that, as a body, they gave themselves to the task of winning Israel to faith in Jesus as the Messiah, but if Jesus had given them, perhaps quite informally, and perhaps not to the Twelve exclusively, the title *sh'luḥin* (in the sense of 'agents')they must have retained it. It is difficult on any other view to account for later developments, and above all for Paul's reference to 'those who were apostles before me' (Gal. 1:17). This means that passages such as Mark 13:10, Matt. 28:19, are to be regarded as developments within the tradition. This will be considered below;[147] it is important because it shows that the word 'apostle' (whether in Greek, Hebrew, or Aramaic), though it originally bore a different meaning, came to be interpreted in the Pauline sense.

The Twelve were not Gentile missionaries; yet somehow the Gentile mission began. There is no reason to think that its beginnings were simple; probably they were not. Some of the hints given by Acts may not be far wide of the mark. It may well be that the Jerusalem group represented by the Seven had something to do with it.[148] It may be that it began by accident through indiscriminate preaching in a place of mixed population like Antioch.[149] Peter was more mobile than his colleagues, as not only Acts but also Gal. 2 suggests; he may well have pursued his apostolate to the Jews[150] into regions where Jews were a minority,[151] and thus have found himself in contact with Gentiles. All these are guesses; what is certain is that a Gentile mission, and with it a Gentile problem, came into being. Both were developed, the mission advanced and the problem exacerbated, by the intervention of Paul, with whom a number of colleagues were associated. This must have happened very early; Paul believed that he was commissioned to this apostolate, which he understood in a missionary sense, in an appearance of the risen Christ belonging to the same series as those granted to Peter and James (1 Cor. 15: 5–8), and this he could not have maintained with any show of plausibility – as it was, the appearance seems to have been questioned – if it had happened long after the appearances were known to have ceased.

Paul, then, was now the leader of another apostolic group, using the Greek word (ἀπόστολος), for their work took them to the Greek-speaking world, but in a sense not unrelated to the Jewish *shaliaḥ*, though, as we have seen, for Paul it meant not 'agent' simply but specifically 'missionary agent', and his understanding of the often-quoted rabbinic dictum, 'A man's *shaliaḥ* is as himself', was (if he thought about it at all) determined by the fact that the person whose *shaliaḥ* he was was Christ crucified, so that his apostleship meant placarding Christ crucified in the sight of the world (Gal. 3: 1) – placarding the crucifixion in his preaching but no less in his person.[152]

Perhaps in part because Paul and his colleagues had taken over the term 'apostle' the leaders of the Jerusalem church – James, Cephas, and John – accepted a new designation for themselves: they were the Pillars (Gal. 2: 9). In part, for there was probably another contributing factor in the ascription to Simon of the name 'Cephas', 'Peter', the 'Rock' (Matt. 16: 18).[153] Whether or not they themselves sanctioned and used the expression 'Supreme Apostles'[154] we cannot tell.

It is well to pause here to note the position that has

now been reached, at (it must be emphasized) a very early period in Christian history. Many reconstructions of the history of the apostolate, and of the use of the term 'apostle', have suffered through oversimplification. It is, of course, natural to try to reduce any situation to its simplest terms, but it is a grand mistake, in the writing of history, to make things simpler than they really were. At this stage we must distinguish between at least eight persons, or groups of persons, all denoted, with varying degrees of propriety, by the term 'apostle' (ἀπόστολος or *shaliaḥ*), and probably all giving it somewhat different meaning. These are:

(1) The original group of (perhaps twelve) messengers or agents whom Jesus had employed in his ministry, and who remained after his death and resurrection as the founder-members of the church in Jerusalem.

(2) Overlapping with these was the smaller group of *Pillars*, or Supreme Apostles, who became the effective leaders of the Jerusalem church. Of these, Peter and John belonged to the Twelve; James did not.

(3) Peter's work took him away from Jerusalem. The Jews were scattered throughout the whole of the Roman Empire, and an 'apostleship of the circumcision' (Gal. 2: 8) could therefore legitimately take him, for example, to Antioch, to Corinth, and to Rome. In doing so it would also create grave problems for him, which this is not the place to discuss; it is, for example, very probable that when Peter left Jerusalem he had not considered what the relations between a circumcised church and an uncircumcised church in Antioch should be, and consequently wavered (Gal. 2: 11–14). We may ask also[155] whether Peter thought of his work as evangelism or as administration. It is quite possible

that as time went on his understanding of apostleship moved in the Pauline direction; to this extent, 1 Peter[156] may not be misleading.

(4) Possibly John's work also took him away from Jerusalem. Of this we cannot be sure, but it would account for the fact that a little later (Acts 21) James is found on his own in Jerusalem, and would be consistent with the second-century tradition that brings John to Ephesus.[157]

(5) The Jerusalem leaders had their own apostles (agents, *sheluḥin*), as non-Christian Jewish authorities in Jerusalem had. These appear (to Paul, in no good light) in Gal. 2: 12, even if they were not the false brothers (2: 4) responsible for perverting the Galatian churches; and in 2 Cor. 10–13 we may perhaps distinguish between – and associate – the false apostles (11: 13) and those who compare themselves with themselves, and boast of what are the labours of other men (10: 12–15). In the Pauline literature we see these men in a controversial light. It must be remembered both that they would have other, in addition to anti-Pauline, activities, and that the existence of false apostles proves the existence of genuine apostles, whom the rest counterfeit. These were probably the apostles of 1 Cor. 15: 7.[158] At their best they represented the Jerusalem church, with its un-Pauline, if not anti-Pauline, tendencies, and could lead Peter out of communion with the Pauline churches; but at their worst they would probably have been repudiated by James as well as by Paul.

(6) There was Paul himself, of whom enough has already been said. He knew that he was an apostle; he knew what it meant to be an apostle. He knew that

the nature of apostleship was bound up with the substance of the Gospel, and if he understood the Gospel
differently from some of his contemporaries, he must
have understood apostleship differently too. There is
clear evidence that this was in fact so.

(7) Just as there were subordinate apostles attached
to the Jerusalem church, so there were others who appear
in Paul's circle. He never claims to be superior to them;
if he had done so, he would have been contradicting
his own understanding of the meaning of apostleship,
since to him an apostle was a servant (2 Cor. 1: 24;
4: 5). But we can hardly think that Paul stood back
while Andronicus and Junias (Rom. 16: 7) took the
lead; Barnabas[159] was more nearly on his own level.[160]
The relation of these men to 1 Cor. 15: 7 is obscure;
it must be remembered that in that passage Paul is
quoting a tradition which he did not himself formulate
and might have expressed differently.

(8) Finally there were the 'apostles of churches'
(2 Cor. 8: 23; Phil. 2: 25), simple delegates or messengers, for whom, however, the same word, 'apostle', was
used.

This complicated and confused state of things
obtained in the first Christian generation. Life often is
confused and complicated, and this makes the lot of
the historian a hard one. But the historian has no
business to complain. He has chosen to record and
interpret life, and life goes on in its complicated way;
it did so in the first century. The preachers preached,
men and women were converted to Christ, their lives
were renewed, they were built up in churches, and these
in turn proceeded to propagate the faith by which they
lived. Two further things, however, may be said about

this generation. (*a*) Inevitably it was marked by tension. The contemporary documents (that is, the Pauline letters) bear clear witness to this, and we need not look at the evidence again. Tension is perhaps too mild a word for the relations between Paul and the Jerusalem headquarters, and we do not know the end of the story of which we have hints in Galatians and 2 Corinthians, and perhaps elsewhere.[161] We do know, however, with a fair measure of probability, (*b*) that the generation closed with the martyrdoms of Paul,[162] Peter,[163] and James[164] – not impossibly, though improbably, also of John,[165] the third of the Pillars. This fact entailed its own problems: the first generation had passed, and the Son of man had not appeared in glory with the clouds of heaven;[166] but it must also have caused thoughtful men to reflect on the disputes that had, at least from time to time, separated these great Christian men, and embittered the relations between them. Whatever their differences, and grievously as some of them might have erred, all had died for the same Lord. This created the task of the next generation. It was one that could be tackled in several ways. In brief, and with perhaps some of that oversimplification that I have deprecated, these were as follows:

(1) The author of the Pastorals, and to some extent also Luke, saw the task, and dealt with it, in *personal* terms. The Pastorals are, as we have seen,[167] a defence of Paul: he is the great apostle, whose voice must now be heard in the new generation. The true theological tradition runs back primarily to him; he is the model of all apostleship, and thus of every Christian minister. It would be mistaken to infer from the Pastorals' silence with regard to other apostles that the author

believed Paul to have been the only true apostle; we have no ground for thinking him a Marcionite. But it would be fair to conclude that for him Paul was so far the standard of the apostolic office that others could be deemed to be apostles if they conformed to that standard. For the author of the Pastorals, the Pauline conception, so far as he understood it, has triumphed.

Acts reaches much the same conclusion, but by a different route. Here there is no question that the Twelve were apostles; but Paul, though systematically described by that title, is at least equally notable as a Christian leader. Acts sees the Twelve as performing a unique function; they are the original apostles appointed by Christ as missionaries, and they thus authorize the Gentile mission by establishing continuity between it and the person and work of Jesus himself. This Paul could not do, because, though he had seen the risen Jesus, he had not accompanied him during his ministry; he is made, however, to replace Peter as the leader of the mission. This looks like what it probably was, a compromise solution. 'The twelve apostles' became a title for the original Jerusalem authorities, but Paul was recognized and depicted as the leader of the advance. As we saw,[168] 1 Peter achieves a similar result by making Peter look like Paul, or at least like an apostle of the Pauline type. The synoptic gospels also have their place here, for they too treat the Twelve as Gentile missionaries, like Paul.[169]

(2) Jude, 2 Peter, and some later writers,[170] see the task of their generation, and deal with it, in *ecclesiastical* terms. The apostles are the fount of the Christian tradition of right doctrine, and the source of commandments

by which Christians must live. Inevitably on this view 'our dear brother Paul' remains a problem and, as a writer of 'Scripture', has to be brought within the orbit of apostolic authority by the principle that Scripture is not of private interpretation. The argument of Tertullian's *De Praescriptione*[171] is implicitly anticipated; the Valentinians, for example, have no right to claim the apostle as their authority – they must be interpreting him wrongly; Marcion has no right to separate Paul from the other apostles;[172] rightly – that is, officially – understood, all are in complete agreement.[173]

(3) John[174] approaches his task in *theological* terms, inquiring into the nature of the apostolic testimony, the authority inherent in it, and the transmission of that authority. I have already indicated the way in which John handles the theological questions with which he was concerned, and here it is necessary only to point out that his answer to them is essentially Paul's answer, though it is cast in a form that Paul could not have employed because it became possible only in the generation after his death. The mark of the disciple is love (John 13: 34f.; 15: 12), expressed in unity with his fellows (17: 11, 21) and faithfulness to the word of Jesus (see above) and to that which he had seen in the life of the incarnate word. Paul is not mentioned;[175] several of the Twelve are mentioned, but it is Paul who gives John the lead in his thinking about the apostles. The word 'apostle' does not occur in its technical sense in either the gospel or the epistles, but these works are full of the theme of apostleship, if apostleship is understood in the Pauline manner.

Only the specifically theological task[176] remains,

and John has prepared the way for it. The best way, however, to approach it will be to return to the synoptic gospels. These undoubtedly reflect, as we should expect, tendencies that we know to have been at work in and just after the apostolic age. There is, for example, as we saw at an earlier stage of our study,[177] the same insistence on the significant number twelve: there are so many apostles, and there cannot be more – whatever we are to make of Paul. It is, of course, relatively easy to deal with the problem of Paul in a gospel: it is unnecessary, indeed it would be anachronistic, to mention him. But it is worth noting that Luke is careful not to describe the Seventy, whose mission is in other respects closely similar to that of the Twelve, as apostles.[178] Beyond this, two important developments are to be noted. (*a*) The Twelve become powerful administrative officers.

Whatever you bind on earth shall be bound in heaven. Whatever you loose on earth shall be loosed in heaven.

'Binding' and 'loosing' are to be understood as rabbinic technical terms[179] which mean 'forbidding' and 'permitting'. That is, the saying means: Your judgements in matters of conduct and law[180] will receive ultimate, divine ratification. This promise is made first to Peter (Matt. 16: 19) and then extended (18: 18) to the church as a whole.[181] (*b*) The Twelve are entrusted with the Gentile mission, which, as we have seen,[182] they did not execute – not through negligence or disobedience, but apparently because they never thought it incumbent upon them, and indeed were doubtful whether it ought to be done at all. Matthew combines the commission with a command to baptize, and with an emphasis upon the teaching authority of the Twelve:

Go and make disciples of all the nations, baptizing them into the name of the Father and of the Son and of the Holy Spirit, teaching them to observe all the things I have commanded you (Matt. 28: 19f.).

Luke similarly incorporates matters of special interest to him:

Thus it is written that the Christ should suffer and on the third day rise from the dead, and that repentance leading to the forgiveness of sins should be preached in his name to all the nations – and you must begin from Jerusalem. You are witnesses of these things (Luke 24: 46ff.).

The longer ending of Mark,[183] representing the latest stage of the tradition, has the plainest of commands:

Go into all the world, and proclaim the Gospel to all creation (Mark 16: 15).

Undoubtedly there was a tendency at work to build up the Twelve as the sole authorized agents of Jesus in the proclamation of the Gospel, and in the administration, education, and discipline of the church. They are figures of glory and power, armed with the unfailing aid of the Spirit (Mark 13: 11 and parallels), and with the supernatural, miracle-working presence of Christ himself (Matt. 18: 19f.; 28: 19f.; Mark 16: 17f.).

A second glance at the gospels reveals a different picture. To become a close disciple of Jesus is to receive a death sentence. Not only are James and John informed that there are no bookable seats in glory, they are told:

The cup that I drink, you shall drink, and with the baptism I am baptized with, you shall be baptized (Mark 10: 39).

It is but a wider application of this when the conditions of discipleship are laid down:

If anyone wishes to come after me, let him deny himself and take up his cross; so let him follow me (Mark 8: 34),

and those who leave everything for Jesus receive the uncomfortable promise,

There is no one who has left household or brothers or sisters or mother or father or children or lands for my sake and for the sake of the Gospel, but shall receive a hundred-fold now in this age, households and brothers and sisters and mothers and children and lands – with persecutions (Mark 10: 29f.).

In a different sector of the Gospel tradition[184] a would-be disciple is warned:

Foxes have earths, the birds of the heaven have nests, but the Son of man has nowhere to lay his head (Matt. 8: 20; Luke 9: 58),

with the clear implication that the followers of the Son of man may expect no better circumstances. Here and there the predictions become more explicit. Discipleship will lead to division within families:

A man's enemies will be the members of his own household (Matt. 10: 36).

The apparatus of persecution will be applied:

Look out for yourselves; they will hand you over to councils and synagogues, you shall be beaten, and you shall stand before governors and kings for my sake (Mark 13: 9).

This persecution, as the last of the Beatitudes reminds us, constitutes the blessedness of the disciples (Matt.

5: 10ff.), and reading back through the Beatitudes we find depicted men who are meek and lowly, peaceable, humble and poor. They are to answer violent opposition by turning the other cheek (Matt. 5: 39; Luke 6: 29), and they are not to exalt themselves over fellow-disciples.

You know that those who are supposed to rule over the nations lord it over them, and their great men exercise authority over them. It is not like that among you. But whoever wishes to become great among you shall be your servant, and whoever wishes to be first among you shall be slave of all (Mark 10: 42ff.).[185]

The Pharisees

love the best place in feasts, and the seats of honour in the synagogues, and greetings in the market places, and to be called Rabbi by men. But do not you be called Rabbi, for you have one teacher, and you are all brothers; and call no one your father on earth, for you have one Father, the heavenly one; and do not be called teachers, for you have one teacher, Christ (Matt. 23: 6–10).[186]

No group of disciples, even the closest, has the right to outlaw another who is able to cast out demons in the name of Jesus (Mark 9: 38ff.).

This is the Pauline attitude to apostleship, expressed in different terms,[187] and its recurrence here is of the first importance. The preservation of this material,[188] in the face of other tendencies whose existence we have noted, marks the essential victory of Paulinism, at a time when Paul's influence might well have seemed to be minimal.[189] It also indicates the real continuity between Jesus and Paul; here, if anywhere, and not in the simple kind of continuity suggested by Acts, is to be found the real connection between Jesus and the church. The complex historical event of crucifixion and resurrection shattered many possible kinds of continuity,[190] but it could serve only to cement together the pattern of crucifixion and resurrection in the teaching, and in the life and death, of Jesus, and the same pattern in the theology and apostolic practice of Paul. Others might be better exponents than Paul of the historical tradition of the words and deeds of Jesus; he perpetuated that in the work of Jesus which was as true and relevant (and of course as offensive and unacceptable) in the Gentile world as in Palestine, that which was independent of the validity of any apocalyptic timetable – including those of Jesus and Paul themselves. To live by faith in the unqualified sovereignty and grace of God; to discharge a debt to the privileged and unprivileged, to the religious and the irreligious; to face error with strength and pride with meekness: this was to carry about in an apostolic ministry the dying and the rising of the dead and risen Jesus.

It is clear that we have reached the point at which we may reasonably ask, and hope to answer, our second question: What is an apostolic church?

The Apostolicity

of the Church

The Apostolicity

of the Church

WHAT are the marks by which the true, authentic church of Christ may be discerned? What characteristics distinguish its faith and order, its preaching and its life?

If the examination of apostles and apostleship in the New Testament, and especially in the story of Paul, that we have now conducted, means anything at all, it should tell us at once that there is no simple formula by which the new question can be answered. There is no simple, rigid definition of apostolicity, just as there is no simple, rigid definition of an apostle. If you had lined up a suitable first-century identification parade you would have found no distinctive marks by which to pick out Paul as an apostle, nor did he carry with him letters or orders to establish his ecclesiastical status. There was moreover in his day no established canon of orthodoxy by means of which his beliefs and teaching might be checked, nor was there any universal church framework into which he could be required to fit. There were indeed attempts[191] to construct canons of behaviour and church relationship, and to show that Paul did not fit into them and could not therefore be a satisfactory apostle: he did not carry letters of commendation from the right quarters (2 Cor. 3: 1), he was not an imposing personality, or an impressive speaker (2 Cor. 10: 1, 10). We know the sort of treatment Paul gave to that sort of attack (for example, 2 Cor. 10: 2–6). In the end, however, he was left with his own conviction, and little to confirm it. He knew that he had seen the risen Christ; what else could have ended his career as a persecutor?[192] But he could not prove it; the date of the supposed event seemed to prove the falsehood of his claim;[193] and it appears that, when he wrote 2 Cor. 12, in the midst of his career, he had to go back fourteen years to find the kind of visionary experience that could revive and confirm his own conviction. He had the seal of his apostleship in the converts he had won (1 Cor. 9: 2; 2 Cor. 3: 2); but when he looked at Corinth he must sometimes at least have doubted the reality of their conversion.[194] He had received in Jerusalem the recognition of the authorities whom men deemed to be pillars (Gal. 2: 9); but hardly had he left Jerusalem for Antioch when one pillar (James) had sent a message of rebuke[195] to another (Peter) with the result that they had virtually excommunicated Paul along with his Gentile churches (Gal. 2: 12).

So much by way of resumption of what I have already said. Whatever Paul may have meant by 'the signs of an apostle',[196] there were no observable proofs that could demonstrate his apostolic status in such a way as to bring automatic conviction to an impartial observer. And the same was true of the rest, even of the 'super-apostles', whether they liked it or not; for, as 2 Cor. 11: 22 shows that whatever qualifications they could claim Paul could claim too; and if in his case these did not amount to proof, neither did they in theirs. Let us add this: Jesus himself was in no better position. Whatever the truth about the person of Jesus is, he himself failed to find means of proving it to the satisfaction of his hearers – this, at least, is indisputable historical fact, for if it had not been so there would have been no crucifixion. Further, he does not appear even to have made any serious effort to prove it. Read the earliest gospel, Mark, and ask where and when Jesus publicly claimed to be the Messiah. The answer is, once only, and that in circumstances that cannot be historically verified,[197] and if they could were such that no one could have believed him – in the Sanhedrin, on trial for his life, in answer to the High Priest's question (Mark 14: 61f.). As to when and where Jesus publicly claimed to be the Son of God, the answer is the same. These two negative statements must not be misunderstood. They relate to public pronouncements, and do not and cannot mean that Jesus was, and believed himself to be, nothing more than man. Jesus made in fact the clearest possible claim to unique authority: he used it, and if he refused to define it (Mark 11: 33), and abstained from using current categories of authority (such as Messiahship), this was primarily because they were too small for him, not because they were too big. The fact is that he was content to go on doing the task he had received from the Father, without concerning himself over questions of status; nor indeed was there anything he could do to establish his status publicly. It was useless, for example, to point to miracles at a time when miracles were two-a-penny, and could in any case be ascribed to the prince of the demons.[198] He could only continue to live in the service of the outcast (for example, Mark 2: 16), and in the confident hope of the kingdom (for example, Mark 1: 15), and, when the time came, die in the same cause.[199]

These things being so, it will hardly be profitable to look for infallible and unmistakable marks of apostolicity in the church. Any claim to possess such marks will be suspicious rather than convincing. A church order that claims to represent the one true apostolic form of the church will not only fail to do justice to the variety found in the New Testament,[200] it will run the risk of being more apostolic than the apostles, or, more accurately, will be seen to adopt an attitude from which the apostles had to be drawn away.[201] The church lives by faith, not by its own form, and the seal of its apostolicity is to be found not in its order but in the sinners it has won from wickedness to God, and in the needy it has comforted, healed, and helped.

Nor is the pious cultivation of an orthodox formula, whether it comes from Chalcedon, Augsburg, or Westminster,[202] an infallible sign of apostolicity. Few were so careless of orthodox formulas as Jesus,[203] and there is something more than a little precious in affecting a greater concern for orthodoxy than his. He asked for loyalty to himself, not to a creed – his closest followers might well have been insufficiently intelligent to understand a creed if he had offered them one,[204] and though in the end their loyalty broke (Mark 14: 50), so far as it went it was genuine, and the decisive matter.[205] He expected the sick who wished to be cured to believe in him, that is, in his power and will to do what they needed (for example, Mark 2: 5; 5: 28; 9: 24);[206] he did not ask what they believed about him.[207] He directed his mission primarily to those who were least sound in the Jewish religion.[208] It would be possible to take the problems of Christology further still, and ask, in all historical seriousness, precisely how much we know about the Jesus of history, and whether it is legitimate to build an exclusive dogmatic superstructure[209] on a rickety historical foundation; but this, I think, is not the vital point, and there is no room to treat it in this lecture.

No church can claim to be authentically the church of Jesus Christ, can demonstrate its apostolicity, by pointing to its church order or to its dogmatic formularies. Does this mean that we are all free to do as we like, and believe as we please? To draw this conclusion would be as false to the New Testament as to suppose that order and orthodoxy can in themselves demonstrate apostolicity. There is no one apostolic church order; but Paul knew that the Lord had given him authority – to be used for building up, not throwing down[210] – and he urged his churches to show due deference to those whom the Lord called as their leaders.[211] Disorderliness was no virtue,[212] though he could be very patient with it. There was no creed available for subscription;[213] but not even an angel had the right to tamper with the Gospel (Gal. 1: 8f.), and the Romans could be reminded that they had been committed to a pattern of teaching (Rom. 6: 17).

There were marks that distinguished the ministry of the apostles and their teachings,[214] though they were not the kind of mark that could automatically vindicate them in the eyes of an impartial and uncommitted observer. In the same way, though there is no church order, and no orthodox formulation of belief, by which the apostolicity of the church can be established, there are marks which the church can and should look for in itself if it means seriously to be the church of Christ.

In part, these are negative. A church that is exclusive

is not truly an apostolic church, a church of Jesus Christ. 'Receive one another, as Christ received you' is Paul's word to a divided church at Rome (Rom. 15: 7), and we know the terms on which Christ received men. He had a name for eating with the outcast and disreputable (for example, Mark 2: 16), and there is no reason to think that he has changed his ways, and no reason why we should be more careful of the company we keep. To exclude from communion not simply the sinful but the Christian who happens to practise a different kind of order from ours is not apostolicity but a double betrayal of Christ. As E. Käsemann has said,[215] 'Christ comes to the godless, even on Sunday morning'.[216] At the same time, a church is not apostolic if it fails to exercise discipline over its members. To accept the returning sinner, to invite and bring him home, is one thing; to cherish the wilful and persistent offender is another. It is, however, important to know what a wilful and persistent offender is. He is not one (if in this we are to follow Paul's example) who flouts authority;[217] he is one who has rejected the law of love.[218] Such a one can only be handed over to Satan, not indeed for damnation but for discipline.[219] Manifestly he does not 'love the Lord', or he would not disobey his command; and not to 'love the Lord' is Paul's one ground for exclusion.[220]

Again, a church is not apostolic if it fails to manifest concern for the needy, and to serve them in love. The one great corporate act of the Pauline churches was the collection, the ministry,[221] for the poor in Jerusalem.[222] We can press further back than this: past the Jerusalem church's own concern for its own poor,[223] to the 'Why call ye me Lord, Lord, and do not the things that I say?' of the Lord's sermon (Luke 6: 46; cf. Matt. 7: 21), and the grim picture of the Judgement, in which those who have not cared for Christ in the person of his hungry, naked, sick, imprisoned, alien brothers, depart into everlasting fire (Matt. 25: 41, 46).

It is perhaps not ridiculous to add, as the last of these negative observations, that a church is not apostolic if it is not apostolic – that is, if it does not enter into the mission that the Lord entrusts to his people. 'Are all apostles?' Paul asked, clearly expecting the answer No;[224] that is, all are not wandering missionaries, who go from place to place to preach and found Christian societies. All are not apostles, but it is the church as a whole that has inherited the commission, 'As the Father has sent me, so I send you' (John 20: 21), and it is the church as a whole, with its infinite variety of personal gift and equipment, that fulfils the commission. The nature of the task will vary from age to age and from place to place, and the church's organization, structure, and method must change to meet changing circumstances; indeed, changing, adaptable structures might be said to be a better mark of apostolicity than an order received from remote ages and carefully preserved. Readiness and fitness for the evangelistic mission, and – as it may not be superfluous to add in these days, when 'mission' is a vogue word but all too seldom a practical programme – the actual carrying out of the evangelistic mission, are true apostolicity.

I have already begun to move from negative to positive marks of apostolicity. The step may be completed if we bear in mind that Paul's understanding of apostleship, backed up by the teaching and example of

Jesus, and coming to prevail in the New Testament as a whole,[225] can be summed up as the carrying about of the dying of Jesus.[226] The same condition applies to the apostolicity of the church.

This principle may be seen, first, in the church's life. It should be seen in sacrificial giving, and service; and if I do not develop this point at length it is because others have done so more eloquently than I could, and with greater first-hand knowledge of the facts of world need. The church (where it is the true, apostolic church) devotes itself to this need, not to win converts, not to gain credibility, not to check communism, but simply because if it did not do so it would no longer be the church. The same principle, however, should be seen also in the way in which the church conducts its affairs; here it is perhaps more necessary to make the point. There is no room in a truly apostolic church that takes seriously its responsibility to carry about the dying of Jesus, and to represent Christ crucified to the world, for the 'great minister' (an odd contradiction in terms) or prelate. There is no nobler Christian title than '*servus servorum Dei*',[227] but whether this has been best exemplified by those who have officially borne it is a question that few today would regard as an open one.[228] What Christ asks of his disciples is whether they are prepared to carry their crosses after him, and though it is true that for some this may mean bearing the burdensome responsibility of leadership in the community of Christians[229] it is not a badge of superiority in a human sense. Those who leave all to follow Christ receive in this age, with persecutions, a hundredfold, mothers, brothers, and sisters (Mark 10: 30); they are not promised a multitude of inferior dependants.

Equally, they are promised no security in a human sense: they are offered only the utter insecurity of the Cross, which becomes security only because they share it with Jesus; and even he experienced it not as security but as despair: 'My God, my God, why hast thou forsaken me?'[230] The commission, 'As the Father has sent me, so send I you' (John 20: 21), is not a charter of privilege and authority, but condemnation to the Cross – how else did the Father send the Son? In other words, an apostolic church will live by faith – faith that is not qualified by sight, faith that becomes operative in love. This faith is directed not towards its own order or orthodoxy, but towards God, who raises the dead and calls being out of non-being. Hence the church that lives by faith lives also by the power of God. God's creative action is not always visible; too often it is obscured by the church's unbelief and pride; in any case, we do not yet live in heaven. But if the 'antepast of heaven' is not available to us now, it is through our own fault, and we are so far lacking in apostolicity. The righteousness, peace, and joy of the kingdom of God are anticipated in the work of the Holy Spirit (Rom. 14: 17).

The same mark of apostolicity that appears in the church's life is seen also, secondly, in the church's preaching.

We preach Christ crucified (1 Cor. 1: 23).
Foolish Galatians, who has bewitched you, before whose eyes Jesus Christ was placarded as crucified? (Gal. 3: 1).

If in Corinth Paul was resolved to know nothing but Christ, and him crucified (1 Cor. 2: 2), this was not because he had just come off badly with philosophy in

Athens, but because he had nothing else to preach. It is not every part of the New Testament that says this with Paul's epigrammatic vehemence, but every part of the New Testament, from Matthew to Revelation,[231] practises it; the gospels, which leave out so much that we inquisitive biographers would like to know about Jesus, do not fail to tell the story of the Cross, in all the detail they can muster; Hebrews develops the imagery of the High Priest who is also victim; I Peter (2: 22–25) quotes Is. 53; John insists that Jesus came not with the water only but with the water and the blood (1 John 5: 6); in Revelation it is the blood of the Lamb slain from the foundation of the world that is the source of cleansing and victory, and the Lamb shares in the worship given to God (Rev. 7: 9f., 14; 12: 11). A church can afford to condone a good deal of eccentricity in its preaching if in the end the preaching focuses on this point. Preaching that does this may be neither learned nor eloquent, but it will not fail in the essentials.

(1) It will rest upon the true historical foundations of Christianity. 'Christ crucified' is a meaningless formula unless we know something at least of the Jesus who was crucified. To tell the story of the Cross drives you, as the evangelists found,[232] into the story of the ministry, and the record of him who made available to men a way to God that did not rest upon the law and therefore applied not only to the religious and virtuous but to all. And to preach the Cross is to preach the resurrection. 'Christ is risen in his word', as the saying goes today. It is not, perhaps, the clearest of theological pronouncements. It is best taken (though whether this would please all who use it I cannot say) in the sense of the dictum of the Reformers: *Praedicatio*

verbi divini est verbum divinum, 'the preaching of God's word is God's word'; that is, when in God's mercy there takes place 'a manifestation of the Incarnate Word, from the Written Word, by the spoken word',[233] then the incarnate word, the Son of God, truly is present, and truly is alive. In this way men who cannot hope to verify the emptiness of the tomb, or even to enjoy 'resurrection appearances', may be convinced of the Easter message and encounter the risen Jesus. No one would preach Christ crucified as Lord, if God had not vindicated Jesus and his work, and the very fact of preaching is thus a mark of the resurrection – a mark, however, but only a mark; the truth of the resurrection lies elsewhere, and preaching manifests it.

(2) Such preaching is bound up with essential dogmatics. This is not to say that all preachers will be good theologians (though the better they are, the healthier the church will be). It means that the preacher is the visible – audible – part of the whole, and from what appears the total structure can be inferred: *ex pede Herculem*. From what I have just said – the centrality in preaching of the Cross, and the coherence with it of the ministry and resurrection of Jesus – the essentials of Christian theology can be reconstructed, for this is the one source of our knowledge both of God and of man and of the relation between God and man. These are not discovered by speculation, but by looking at Jesus. The doctrine of God is here, for the God whom no man has ever seen is set forth in the Son who shares his being (John 1: 18); the truth about man is revealed in the Son of man who recovered man's lordship in and over creation through the obedience for which man was created (Ps. 8); the doctrine of grace, though

of course it needs elaboration, is pictured in the friend of publicans and sinners (Matt. 11: 19; Luke 7: 34); the duty and joy of gratitude as the spring of ethical response are present, for example, in the parable of the debtors (Matt. 18: 23–35; cf. Luke 7: 41–48). God, man, grace, gratitude: what Barth has done in a dozen volumes of Dogmatics cannot be done here in half-a-dozen lines, but it is done, in essence, in every true preaching of Christ crucified.

(3) Such preaching will be effective preaching, converting preaching. For the Cross is judgement; there is nothing that so calls in question not only the surface conventionalities but all the subterranean prejudices of human life, nothing so likely to strip a man naked and leave him exposed, in the first instance before his own looking-glass, and then in the sight of God.

> When I survey the wondrous Cross,
>   Where the young Prince of glory died,
> My richest gain I count but loss,
>   And pour contempt on all my pride.

You may, if you will, say that the Cross means a radical, existential questioning of all the presuppositions of my being. This is true, and well said, though as English it is not so perspicuous as Watts's. What is meant is the first step to that reorientation of life in which egocentricity is exchanged for theocentricity, the new life in which I am crucified to the world, the life I live in the flesh by faith in the Son of God who loved me and gave himself for me (Gal. 2: 20; 6: 14).

The challenge to the church's apostolicity is seen already in the New Testament, especially as the challenge to Paul's apostleship, and his conception of apostleship. Some of the details of this were studied earlier in this lecture.[234] Sometimes the challenge was an attack from without,[235] sometimes it was, more subtly, perversion from within.[236] Already in the New Testament we see apostles being built up as ecclesiastical bureaucrats (for example, Matt. 16: 19) and the guardians of tradition (for example, Matt. 28: 20a), and in Diotrephes (3 John 9ff.) we may recognize the less endearing features of church dignitaries. The gnostic crisis – or, better, the gnostic war of attrition, for it lasted from New Testament times to the end of the second century – completed the perversion.[237]

Gnosticism, or gnosis,[238] is not easy to define in a few words, or, for that matter, in many. More important, perhaps, than any propositional definition of its intellectual content, which included Oriental and Hellenistic, religious and philosophical elements, is the fact that it pervaded the Near East in the time of the New Testament. It was an atmosphere, a fashion, a habit of thought, that most men absorbed like the air they breathed, while others revolted against it as a poisonous gas. In its basic principles it was akin to astrology, for it shared the conviction that the affairs of men were determined by heavenly bodies, so that only those who could escape through the spheres might hope for apotheosis and immortality; and it had something in common with the cult of the 'divine man',[239] in that it was a Gospel, a message that could be apprehended and proclaimed only by men of exceptional, perhaps of more than human, insight and wisdom. It could not but be a problem for Christians, because it was so like Christianity, and at the same time so radically different. It was like Christianity in that it proclaimed one God, who willed to reveal himself to men, a God in knowledge of whom stood their salvation and eternal life; it was unlike, in that the knowledge, *gnosis*, which brought salvation, was mystically and mythically, and not historically, conveyed, and meant the accumulation of cosmic secrets rather than an interrogation and revaluation of the self.[240] Gnosticism, moreover, was regularly dualistic, so that creation rather than salvation was always its problem: why should a God, who by definition is spiritual and therefore good, create a universe that is at least partly material and therefore at least partly evil? Salvation could be readily explained as the separation of the spiritual from the material, that the former might be free; but how did the two come to be mixed up? In practice gnosis led to, indeed it was, speculative theology, and in ethics its dualism was expressed either in an ascetic attitude to life, or in licentious indifferentism.[241]

That gnosis of a sort was in existence as early as Christianity is beyond dispute. The notion that salvation comes through knowledge is Platonic,[242] and so is a form of dualism; equally these beliefs appear in oriental religions of considerable antiquity. More important, perhaps, as proof that gnosis is antecedent to or at least contemporary with the New Testament, is the fact that parts of the New Testament make better sense if one may suppose that they were written against a gnostic background. Undoubtedly, for example, there were in Corinth some who claimed to possess a superior knowledge, by which they could regulate their conduct (1 Cor. 8: 1, 7, 10, 11); Paul's response was not to deny the existence of such knowledge and wisdom (1 Cor. 12: 8 – it could be a gift of God), but to insist on the supremacy of love (1 Cor. 13: 2, 13), and to point out the true nature of Christian wisdom (1 Cor. 2: 6-9). Equally clear indications are to be found in, for example, Colossians (2: 3, 8, 16ff., 21ff.) and 1 John (2: 4; 3: 6; 4: 6ff.; 5: 20); but it is not my purpose here to discuss gnosis (or gnosticism) in the New Testament, but simply to note its existence.[243]

At the other end of the scale, gnosticism as a fully developed Christian heresy is to be found in the middle of the second century. Among its great exponents were Valentinus, Basilides, Carpocrates, and, paradoxically (for he was also, in a sense, a biblical theologian), Marcion.[244] These men were answered by such Christian theologians as Irenaeus, Hippolytus, and Tertullian, who certainly did not go out of their way to depict gnosticism in the most favourable light. In their refutations it appears as a fantastic mythological scheme of a world populated and controlled by aeons and emanations. The gnosticism that won so strong a following in the latter part of the second century takes on a different, and more comprehensible, appearance in the 'Gospel of Truth',[245] and in the attractive and not unorthodox Clement of Alexandria.[246] Once more, it is impossible for me to go into detail: the one point that we must observe is that gnosticism existed as a phenomenon contemporary with primitive Christianity, partly alongside it and in opposition to it, partly also within it. There was a paradoxical relation between the two, and a standing and unrelaxed tension between the similarities and differences that marked them.

The reactions of Christians to gnosticism were diverse. On the one hand – how 'modern' this is! – there were some who let themselves go in the adaptation of Christian truth to current thinking; on the other, the defenders fell back upon the Maginot line of what they regarded as an apostolic creed, an apostolic ministry and succession, and an apostolic tradition, not perceiving that they were using the adjective 'apostolic' to undermine the true apostolicity of the church. I do not mean that all second-century Christians can be neatly divided into these two camps. It was precisely at this time that the idea of 'orthodoxy' and 'heresy' was being hammered out, and sometimes the same author shows both characteristics. Ignatius, for example, is himself a thinker of a gnostic type, by no means unaffected by astrology; he attacks gnostic teachers of a kind he does not approve; and he develops in opposition to them, and fervently supports, the threefold ministerial institution of bishops, presbyters, and deacons.[247] As, however, the second century wore on, the general tendency was for men to separate themselves into groups, dominated respectively by freedom of speculation, and by firm maintenance of the institutional framework of the church.

Both groups appealed to the apostles. The gnostic literature is full of allusion to the apostolic literature of the New Testament. 'Their method of expression can be said to be entirely orientated around the Scriptures.'[248] It is true, as Gärtner shows in this context, that the gnostic writers often proceed by way of allusion rather than by clear quotation, and that their exegesis is frequently forced. He quotes an excellent passage from Tertullian, who complains that, whereas only Marcion actually excised parts of the New Testament, others might treat Scripture with as little respect.

One man perverts Scripture with his hand, another with his exegesis. If Valentinus seems to have used the whole Bible, he laid violent hands upon the truth with just as much cunning as Marcion. Marcion openly and nakedly used the knife, not the pen, massacring Scripture to suit his own material. Valentinus spared the text, since he did not invent Scriptures to suit his matter, but matter to suit the Scriptures. Yet he took more away, and added more, by taking away the proper meanings of particular words and by adding fantastic arguments (Tertullian, *De Praescriptione* 38).

To the gnostics, the apostolic writers were authoritative because they themselves were gnostics *par excellence*, endowed with the divine spark of knowledge, and indeed more than human.

After the resurrection, when he breathed the Spirit into the apostles (John 20:22), he blew away and separated off the earthy like ash, and kindled the spark and quickened it (*Excerpta ex Theodoto* 3.2).[249]

The apostles were changed into [this rendering is uncertain] the twelve signs of the Zodiac; for as generation is ordered by the latter, so regeneration is superintended by the former (*Exc. ex Theod.* 25.2).

The Saviour taught the apostles in the first place in types and mysteries, in the second place in parables and riddles, and in the third place, when they were alone, plainly and directly (*Exc. ex Theod.* 66).

The last quotation alludes to the time after the resurrection when, it was believed, the Lord disclosed plainly to the apostles those secret traditions which previously had been presented in mysterious form, and constituted the basis and justification of the gnostic interpretation of Scripture. It is important to note that the gnostics had their apostolic tradition, to which they appealed, though knowledge of it was reserved for the elect.

For, if God grants it, you shall learn in due course about the origin and generation of this [the Good], if you are counted worthy of the apostolic tradition (τῆς ἀποστολικῆς παραδότεως), which we too have received by succession (ἐκ διαδοχῆς) (*The Epistle of Ptolemaeus to Flora*, V 10).[250]

It was, at least in part, in opposition to this gnostic development of apostolic teaching and tradition that orthodox[251] Christians developed their own use of Scripture, tradition, and the ministry of authorized teachers. Except with Marcion,[252] there was probably little dispute about the extent of apostolic Scripture (that is, the limits of the canon), and its authority. It was in regard to its interpretation, and the traditional material which both supplemented it and helped to determine its meaning, that conflict arose. The conflict should be observed with sympathy and understanding. Probably there were both good intentions and sharp practice on both sides. The gnostics could claim that they were following the example of freedom set by Paul and John in using the new ways of thinking current in their day. They could claim too that it was not the intention of the apostles to establish a rigid framework of orthodoxy which all Christians of all ages must accept, still less a rigid framework of ecclesiastical organization to which all Christians of all ages must conform. At the same time, they allowed their freedom to become unbridled, and used the most fantastic exegesis to put into the mouths of the apostles thoughts that the apostles cannot possibly have intended.[253] Over against this, the orthodox, though they too allegorized, adopted on the whole a more straightforward kind of exegesis, and (though they might have been content to let their exegesis justify itself by its inherently greater probability) insisted that apostolic tradition was public, not secret, tradition, and must be understood to be confined to the apostolic succession of authorized (episcopal) teachers in the apostolic sees. This was the original,[254] and relatively harmless, sense of apostolic succession; but it has the seeds of legalism in it, and already in the second century the seeds had begun to flower.[255]

There was right and wrong on both sides. Neither unbridled freedom nor hidebound orthodoxy is apostolic Christianity; this in any case is not preserved in and does not flow exclusively along cut-and-dried channels. That which is not a fresh creation of the Spirit is, however orthodox, not apostolic. Gnosticism as a heresy marks the first great lost opportunity of the church; both sides, those whom we call the heretics and those whom we call the orthodox, were so nearly right, and, in different ways, so terribly wrong.[256]

It was a long time before the great second chance came – at least, before a second chance was accepted; so long that the acceptance of it disrupted the church. There is no scope in this lecture for me to tell the story of Christianity from the second century onwards, nor am I competent to tell it. It is a strange mixture of saintliness and sin, of learning and ignorance, of humanity and beastliness, of the word of God and the word of man. All this is not least true of the Middle Ages. I should be the last to depreciate the saints and scholars of this period; but it is not unfair to them to say that it witnessed much misunderstanding and perversion of biblical Christianity, and that its total effect was to bring the people of God into a Babylonian Captivity,[257] in which the disciplined freedom of the apostolic age[258] was exchanged for tyranny. Theology was confined within an Aristotelian prison, souls were directed by law rather than Gospel, and the church was governed by priests and monks – the spiritual estate.[259] I repeat that I am well aware that exceptions could be found to each of these statements; that does not mean that each of them is not broadly true. It remains an essentially simple, even though historically very complex, fact that it was in the Reformation of the sixteenth century that the 'theology of glory'[260] was replaced by the 'theology of the Cross', and the priesthood of the spiritual estate by the priesthood of all God's people. These terms are central, but not easy to define. Luther had already stated the contrast between the two theologies in Conclusio 21 of the Heidelberg Disputation (1518): 'The exponent of the theology of glory (*theologus gloriae*) says that bad is good and good is bad. The exponent of the theology of the Cross (*theologus crucis*) says that which is fact'.[261] Enemies of the Cross of Christ, Luther goes on (alluding to Phil. 3: 18), believe in works and the glory of them; works, which are really evil, they call good, and the good of the Cross they call evil. In itself this sounds like little more than the repetition of a party slogan, but the opening sentence of the *probatio* is more profound: 'Because he [the *theologus gloriae*] does not know Christ, he does not know God as he is hidden in the sufferings (*in passionibus*) [of the Cross].'[262] Medieval theology (again, perhaps, somewhat unfairly judged and generalized) was a theology of glory, because it sought means, rational, mystical, ecclesiastical, of ascending to God in his glory; the theology Luther learned from his New Testament found God – a God, indeed, still hidden (*absconditus*) even when found – in the wounds of Jesus Christianity becomes once more what Paul said it was, a carrying about in our bodies of the dying of Jesus (2 Cor. 4: 10; see above, p. 43). Nor did Luther forget that Paul continues: 'that the life also of Jesus may be manifested in our bodies'; he has a new theology of glory,[263] which arises simply out of the fact that the Christ who was crucified is the same Christ whom God raised from the dead. The whole is perhaps best summed up in the last of the theological conclusions in the Heidelberg Disputation (28), of which Nygren[264] makes so much: 'God's love does not find but makes its object of love (*non invenit sed creat suum diligibile*), man's love is made by its object of love.' This proposition safeguards the truth that God's love is for sinners, and waits upon no desert or value in man; it is the love God commends to us in that while we were still sinners Christ died for us. It equally safeguards the truth that God's love creates within sinners something that is properly an object of love, since Christ is formed in their hearts by faith.

'The priesthood of all believers' has in recent years been defined and counter-defined[265] till most believers must be perplexed by it. This is not the place to expound the biblical passages[266] on which it is based; it may suffice to say that the doctrine means what it says.

Let every man then who has learnt that he is a Christian recognise what he is, and be certain that we are all equally priests; that is, that we have the same power in the word, and in any sacrament whatever; although it is not lawful for any one to use this power, except with the consent of the community, or at the call of a superior. For that which belongs to all in common no individual can arrogate to himself, until he be called.[267]

There is in principle, and in fact, no priestly act that the ordinary Christian may not perform. Luther goes on, however, to show that the primary function of the priesthood is preaching; of the diaconate, the distribution of the church's wealth among the poor. These tasks call for special gifts which not all Christians possess, and not every Christian is the best judge of whether he does in fact himself possess them. Hence the necessity of the community's consent, or call. The sacraments of the Lord's Supper and baptism do not call for the same kind of qualification, but decency and order suggest that not everyone should perform them.[268] There is no indelible character conferred in the supposed sacrament of orders.

I do not see at all for what reason a man who has once been made priest cannot become a layman again, since he differs in no wise from a layman, except by his ministerial office;[269]

-- that is, by the fact that he has been called to preach, to administer the sacraments, and to exercise pastoral care. What Luther is concerned with, however, in the context in which he writes, is levelling up, not levelling down.

He who is a Christian has Christ and he who has Christ has all things that are Christ's, and can do all things (*potens omnia*).[270]

Something at least of the apostolic message and of apostolic freedom had been rediscovered; to recognize that, in the end, with all our learning, piety, and splendour, we are in the presence of God but beggars,[271] is to stand some chance of receiving the riches of his grace.

It did not last; notwithstanding the practical Protestantism of early Methodism, it did not last. Wesley was quite properly capable of criticizing both Luther and Calvin; sometimes, too, he could criticize improperly on the basis of inadequate reading;[272] but he did not question that he stood with them on the major issues.[273] What more *practical* expression of the theology of the Cross can one find than the mission that led through the hills and dales, the slums and alleys, of eighteenth-century England, offering to all without exception, to the most sinful, ignorant and degraded, a full, free, and present salvation? The Christ who had stooped to the Cross could be trusted to come to them, to their coalmines and their hovels, and there to liberate the splendours of redeeming love; and God's love was never more visibly active in creating its lovable object than then. It was the same mystery of divine condescension that Luther had sung in *Nun freut euch, lieben Christen gmein*.

> 'Tis mystery all! The immortal dies;
> Who can explore his strange design?

And the affiliation is made clearest of all in translation:

> Now I have found the ground wherein
> Sure my soul's anchor may remain —
> The wounds of Jesus, for my sin
> Before the world's foundation slain;
> Whose mercy shall unshaken stay,
> When heaven and earth are fled away.[274]

The little man who surrendered the comforts of Oxford for the hardships of the road, and the slings and arrows of an ungrateful establishment, was an apostle of divine love, carrying about in the body the dying of Jesus, an emblem as well as a preacher of the Cross; and he too could have said of himself and his hearers: 'So then death is at work in us, but life in you.'[275]

And what more *practical* expression of the priesthood of all believers has there been than that in which local preachers shared in the proclamation of the Gospel and lay class leaders in the cure of souls? Classical Methodism, with its clerical Conference, undervalued (in comparison with the older Dissent) the role of the layman in governing the church,[276] but it more than made up for this by the place it gave him in the field of spiritual responsibility. Potentially (*potens omnia*) all Christians can do all things; what is needed is the call to execute a particular function. And when Susannah Wesley, Samuel Annesley's daughter, heard Thomas Maxfield preach at the Foundery, she told her son, who was minded to put a stop to the proceedings, 'John, take care what you do with respect to that young man, for he is as surely called of God to preach, as you are. Examine what have been the fruits of his preaching, and hear him yourself.'[277] John could not withstand the evidence of eyes and ears, and the call of the earthly community was added to the divine call.

It did not last, perhaps it never can last; perhaps the dead inertia of human nature is so great that men will always swing back from apostolic Christianity, disciplined and free, into the comfortable but relative securities of order and orthodoxy, whether we call them catholic or ecumenical. Freedom is a costly and painful state to live in. But what we need in the increasingly cosy climate of ecumenical understanding is not to bury but to rediscover the Reformation – not indeed for its own sake, for there is no special virtue in sixteenth-century or in eighteenth-century history, but for the sake of that to which it points us in the New Testament.

We are today in a better position to do this than any of our fathers were; in a better position, perhaps, than when those of us who were studying theology in the 1930s were stirred by the discovery[278] of Barth, and felt ourselves summoned to the work of theology as he described it[279] and to the task of reformation. Little is left of that enthusiasm today. The present is by no means a time of renewed reformation theology,[280] but is in many ways a time of great danger to the Christian faith, a time in which its essential message is threatened not so much by opposition from without (though this is increasingly encountered) as by corruption from within, to the extent that belief in a personal God seems to be in some quarters regarded as an optional requirement in a Christian minister; yet it is also a time of great opportunity, because radical critical and historical study of the New Testament is leading to a radical understanding of the Christian faith. I have used the word 'radical' with some hesitation, because like all great words, such as 'catholic' and 'evangelical', it is liable to abuse, and I have no wish to claim kinship with some who have borne the title 'radical' – I would disclaim it rather. I use the word in its simple sense of 'going down to the roots'. In this sense, the radical study of the New Testament, a study that shirks no issues, and honestly follows the question wherever it may lead, is a function of the doctrine of justification by faith, itself understood in a radical way to mean precisely what it says, namely that justification is received on trust as a mere gift, and that God attaches no strings to it – as if one should say, 'You are justified provided that . . .'. It is one aspect of this general truth that when we read the New Testament there are no forbidden inquiries. We are not justified, provided that our critical scholarship leads us to conclude that not less than $x\%$ of the sayings of Jesus are genuine, and not fewer than $y\%$ of the Pauline epistles authentic. Christian freedom is real freedom, and it is vindicated by the fact that when, in this freedom, we study the New Testament and interrogate it without reserve we find that what it is about is – freedom,[281] and justification by faith.[282]

This is the last lesson we may draw from our study of the apostles in the New Testament, and especially of the central and normative, even though abortive (1 Cor. 15:8), apostle Paul. We have seen[283] that Paul, though given authority for 'building up' (2 Cor. 10:8; 13:10), did not claim that his words should be accepted because of the authority that he who spoke them bore in his own person. This would have inverted the true situation. Such authority as he had he possessed in virtue of the truth of the message that he preached. He could not authenticate his Gospel; his Gospel authenticated him, so far as he was faithful to it.[284] If he himself, unlikely as this might be, should preach a different Gospel he would lose more than his authority (Gal. 1:8f.). The Corinthians might properly seek some proof of the fact that Christ was speaking in Paul (2 Cor. 13:3), except of course that Christ himself did not choose to impose an external authority upon those who heard him. Hence, as von Campenhausen writes,[285]

Thus [the church's] relation to apostolic authority is necessarily determined in a dialectical way. On the one hand, the community remains for ever bound to the original testimony that it received, and therewith also to the original witnesses, the apostles, who transmitted the testimony to the church and guaranteed it; but on the other hand it is, precisely through this testimony, confronted not simply with men but with Christ, and through him it has become 'free'.

Our attitude to the Canon of Scripture should correspond to that of their contemporaries to the apostles. Von Campenhausen in his very illuminating article continues:[286]

The church becomes the apostolic church, that is, it consciously submits itself, together with that which it believes and requires, to the norm of the apostolic preaching of Christ. But in this binding of itself to its origin it feels itself not to be bound with outward ties, but as free – free afterwards as before.

In the New Testament period the problem was to know who were apostles and who were not; the attempt to limit them rigidly to the Twelve, or to the Twelve with Paul, is clearly secondary. It corresponds to this both that the study of the New Testament raises unanswerable literary and historical problems, and that the delimitation of the Canon cannot fail to evoke doubt and uncertainty.[287] The value and apostolic authority of the Canon are no more affected by these problems and doubts than the value and authority of the apostles was objectively diminished by the analogous problems and doubts of first-century Christians. The church's relation to the Canon is determined in the same dialectic manner as its relation, in the first century, to the apostles; that is, the church, though it did not make and cannot unmake the Canon, but is in subjection to it, is entitled to raise the question whether the biblical writers are always equally, and equally clearly, faithful to the subject-matter of their own primary witness.

This is not a matter of permission, but of obligation. The Christian is not asked to consider whether or not he shall be a free man.

For freedom did Christ set us free; stand firm therefore, and do not be again caught in a yoke of bondage (Gal. 5: 1).

If he is something less than a free man, he is something less than a Christian. He has no right to tie himself, his contemporaries, and his descendants to a particular church order, whether venerable or new-fangled,[288] as if the Lord could have no more light to break forth out of his holy word,[289] and as if the apostles were respectfully treated when there is ascribed to them the kind of authority implicit in a succession. He has no right to set the words of Scripture above the common processes of intelligent inquiry, and ascribe to them a sacrosanct character that forbids the application of critical thought, whether in matters of history or of theology. This freedom, however, exists only within the framework of loyalty to the essential apostolic message, for it is the message of the Cross that sets men free, and the life that is marked by the Cross that is free: 'as dying, and behold we live' (2 Cor. 6: 9).

It is here that we find the answer to our initial questions about preaching, dogmatics, and order. We find them in faithfulness to the New Testament, for preaching, dogmatics, and order that are not founded on the New Testament may be very interesting phenomena, but are certainly not Christian; we find them, however, when we approach the New Testament not in the straitjacket of tradition, but in freedom – freedom limited only where it must be limited, by honesty and integrity in relation to its subject-matter. The theme of the New Testament is Christ crucified and risen, and it vindicates itself. The apostolic testimony to Christ crucified and risen is not a halter, but a spur. It is not life-destroying letter, but life-giving Spirit. Preaching and theology do not consist in simply repeating the words of the Bible, nor is the only true church order one that may be read out of the pages of the New Testament (though, it may be added, one that is not to be found there cannot properly be required of any man, and should be adopted only with the greatest hesitation – preferably not adopted at all). The New Testament is neither a set of sermon outlines, nor a volume of dogmatics, nor a corpus of canon law; it is the classic witness to Christ, from which new methods of study will bring ever new light, the witness that provides the measure for our own. And whether we think of preaching, of dogmatics, or of order, there is no better account of apostolicity than the words of Luther:[290]

What does not teach Christ is not apostolic, even though St Peter or St Paul taught it. On the other hand, what preaches Christ, that would be apostolic, even though Judas, Annas, Pilate, and Herod did it.

So there is hope for us.

And hope therefore for the world too; for an

apostolic church does not exist in order to be able to congratulate itself upon its own apostolicity, but as an instrument in God's hand for the service and salvation of men. Such an instrument it can be, so long as it is apostolic, so long, that is, as it does preach Christ to the world. It is perhaps harder in our generation than at earlier times for the church to get away with substitutes for this. Its formulas, dogmatic or ecclesiastical, the up-to-date as much as the old-fashioned, are not impressive; the non-Christian public is not greatly affected by its interest in organized unity, or in organized welfare. There are few places left in the world where the church can speak from strength, and exert a powerful influence in social and national affairs. Yet the existence of violent and vociferous minorities – and these, one suspects, are sometimes shouting to keep their courage up – should not blind us to the mass of mankind, who are ethically lost because they have grown up without clear-cut moral standards, and intellectually lost because they have (very properly) become sceptical about all the panaceas offered them. Yet they still have to live, and they still have to die. If we had the apostolic simplicity to offer them Jesus, free, not from theology, for that would make him meaningless, and us too, but from limited and limiting formulas; free, not from the fellowship of his younger brothers (Rom. 8: 29), for that too would make him meaningless, but from ecclesiastical exclusiveness, and from insistence on ceremony; if we could do this – then the mass of men might still find him to be foolishness and offence (1 Cor. 1: 23), and the church might still be poor, and persecuted, and unimpressive; but the way of hope would stand open.

Notes

1. Stuttgart 1934/1954.

2. 1, pp. 397–448.

3. See especially H. L. Strack and P. Billerbeck, *Kommentar zum Neuen Testament aus Talmud und Midrasch* (Munich 1922–61), **3**, pp. 2ff.

4. That is, the man appointed to act as 'precentor'. See (for the translation also) H. Danby, *The Mishnah* (Oxford 1933), p. 6.

5. *The Church's Ministry* (London 1948), p. 36. Manson's discussion of the apostolate in this book (pp. 31–52) is of first-rate importance.

6. *Apostolat und Predigtamt* (as in n. 1), p. 24.

7. London 1946; pp. 183–303.

8. Op. cit., pp. 36; see also A. Ehrhardt, *The Apostolic Succession in the first two Centuries of the Church* (London 1953).

9. *Supreme Authority* (London 1953).

10. See pp. 110f.

11. *The Apostle and his Message* (Uppsala 1947).

12. 'Der urchristliche Apostelbegriff', **1** (1948), pp. 96–130. See also von Campenhausen's *Kirchliches Amt und geistliche Vollmacht in den ersten drei Jahrhunderten* (Tübingen 1953).

13. 'Apostolos in the New Testament', **2** (1949–50), pp. 166–200. This article contains brief but useful summaries of earlier views of the history of the apostles.

14. 'Paul, the Apostles, and the Twelve', **3** (1950–51), pp. 96–110.

15. Forschungen zur Religion und Literatur des Alten und Neuen Testaments, Neue Folge **59** (Göttingen 1961).

16. Forschungen (as n. 15), Neue Folge **61** (Göttingen 1961).

17. A great deal more could be cited. Here the following may be mentioned: E. Käsemann, 'Die Legitimität des Apostels', *Zeitschrift für die neutestamentliche Wissenschaft und die Kunde der älteren Kirche*, **41** (1942), pp. 33–71 (since reprinted separately: Darmstadt 1946); J. L. Leuba, *L'Institution et l'Événement* (Neuchâtel/Paris 1950); R. R. Williams, *Authority in the Apostolic Age* (London 1950); Studies in Biblical Theology: **32** E. Schweizer, *Church Order in the New Testament* (London 1961); **46** W. Schmithals, *Paul and James* (London 1965); **47** F. Hahn, *Mission in the New Testament* (London 1965); S. Freyne, *The Twelve: Disciples and Apostles* (London 1968; with a useful short bibliography); and the discussions of the apostles and of apostolicity by K. Barth, in *Church Dogmatics*, II, 2, pp. 431–49; IV, 1, pp. 714–25.

18. See K. Barth, *Church Dogmatics*, I, 1, p. 86: 'Starting from the question how men spoke about God in the Church yesterday, dogmatics asks how this should be done tomorrow.' See the whole section, on Dogmatics and Church Proclamation, pp. 79–97.

19. See Daniel T. Jenkins, *The Nature of Catholicity* (London 1942), a book which, as far as my knowledge goes, has had less influence than it deserves. Jenkins's argument, on pp. 21–4, that catholicity *is* apostolicity ('The supreme mark of a Church's catholicity is its acceptance of and continuity with the testimony of the Apostles. To be Catholic the Church must also be Apostolic' – p. 21), is essentially mine, though I should not express myself in the same way about the unity of the New Testament. The requirements of p. 166 ('Discussion between Anglican and Reformed theologians cannot take place in an atmosphere of real confidence until Anglican theologians show signs of having

mastered the argument of the Prolegomena to Barth's *Dogmatic*'), though one might in any case wish to rephrase it today, is still far from fulfilment – indeed the number of Reformed theologians with the desired qualification is probably diminishing; and the hopefulness of p. 164 ('Our common willingness to stand under the discipline of Biblical theology as practised by Hoskyns is the most hopeful and enduring of our points of contact') has petered out.

20. See below, p. 35.

21. 'Son' is not expressed in Greek, and 'brother' is a conceivable though improbable alternative. Alphaeus has often been identified with Cleopas (Luke 24:18) or Clopas (John 19:25) or with both. See, for example, Vincent Taylor, *The Gospel according to St. Mark* (London 1952), on Mark 3:18.

22. Not a Canaanite, or an inhabitant of Cana, but a member of the Zealot party (*Qan'ana*); see Taylor ad loc.

23. See n. 21. Mark presumably thought that Levi and James were brothers (the third pair among the twelve).

24. Unless Bartimaeus, who 'followed him in the way' (Mark 10:52) is to be thought of as a disciple; 'awaiting the kingdom of God' (Mark 15:43) does not imply that Joseph of Arimathaea was a disciple.

25. Mark 2:15, 16, 18, 23; 3:7, 9; 4:34; 5:31; 6:1, 35, 41, 45; 7:2, 5, 17; 8:1, 4, 6, 10, 27, 33, 34; 9:14, 18, 28, 31; 10:10, 13, 23, 24, 46; 11:1, 14; 12:43; 13:1; 14:4, 12, 13, 14, 16, 32; 16:7.

26. Andrew is placed with Peter; Matthew stands after instead of before Thomas.

27. Luke translates Mark's 'Cananaean'; see n. 22.

28. Conceivably 'brother'; see n. 21, and cf. Mark 6:3.

29. Details of various suggestions are conveniently given by Taylor, op. cit., on Mark 3:18.

30. In Mark 3:18, D it have 'Lebbaeus'. In Matt. 10:3, D k Or[lat] have 'Lebbaeus'; many MSS harmonize, with

'Lebbaeus surnamed Thaddaeus', or 'Thaddaeus surnamed Lebbaeus'; it has 'Judas Zelotes'.

31. See below, pp. 31–4, 67–73.

32. See 21:2; this chapter is almost certainly a supplement to the gospel. The reference may be a hint that the 'beloved disciple' (21:7, 20) should be identified with John. See n. 34.

33. At 6:71; 13:2, 26 (with some textual variation) Simon Iscariot is mentioned as the father of Judas the traitor. One possible interpretation of Iscariot derives the name from *sicarius*; this would make it almost an equivalent of Cananaean and Zealot.

34. There is an excellent account of the various possibilities in R. E. Brown, *The Gospel according to John I–XII* (New York 1966), pp. xciv–xcviii.

35. Luke (10:38–42) mentions two sisters called Mary and Martha, and the Lucan parable of the Rich Man (16:19–31) mentions the poor man Lazarus.

36. Matt. 10:5; 26:14, 47; Mark 3:16; 4:10; 6:7; 9:35; 10:32; 11:11; 14:10, 17, 20, 43; Luke 8:1; 9:1, 12; 18:31; 22:3, 47; John 6:67, 70, 71; 20:24; Acts 6:2; 1 Cor. 15:5.

37. Matt. 26:14, 47; Mark 14:10, 43; Luke 22:3, 47; John 6:71.

38. See W. G. Kümmel, *Kirchenbegriff und Geschichtsbewusstsein in der Urgemeinde und bei Jesus*, Symbolae Biblicae Upsalienses **1** (Zürich/Uppsala 1943), p. 31. Some take this to be a post-resurrection saying.

39. So E. Haenchen, *Der Weg Jesu* (Berlin 1966), p. 138.

40. Cf. Schweizer (as in n. 17) 71; 3n.

41. In Greek the name is *Petros*, the word for rock, *petra*; in Aramaic, *Kepha* serves for both.

42. Here the reconstruction of the underlying Aramaic (or Hebrew) is more difficult. It need not be discussed here; see Taylor, op. cit., on Mark 3:17.

43. Gal. 2:12; see below, p. 38.

44. See N. A. Dahl, in *Studia Theologica* **5** (1952), pp. 160-4.

45. Matt. 4: 18-22; Mark 1: 16-20, 29-31; 13: 3.

46. Convincingly argued by Schweizer (as in n. 17), 2 a b d.

47. E. Meyer, *Ursprung und Anfänge des Christentums* **1** (Stuttgart/Berlin 1921), pp. 133-47, distinguished a 'disciple-source' and a 'Twelve-source'. For criticism of this view see Taylor, op. cit., pp. 74f.

48. As if Mark had said οἱ ἀποσταλέντες, or οἱ ἀπεσταλμένοι.

49. There is a good discussion of the matter in Haenchen, *Der Weg Jesu*, pp. 428f.

50. *The Teaching of Jesus* (Cambridge 1935), p. 394.

51. 'Apostles' (ἀποστόλους); 'send' (ἀποστέλλῃ). So, e.g., Mosbech (n. 13), p. 184.

52. E.g. J. Wellhausen, *Das Evangelium Marci* (Berlin 1909), p. 44; R. Bultmann, *Die Geschichte der synoptischen Tradition*, Forschungen zur Religion und Literatur des Alten und Neuen Testaments, Neue Folge **12** (Göttingen 1931), pp. 155f.

53. 8: 14; 9: 32, 39; 10: 1—11: 18; 12: 17; 15: 7.

54. 1 Cor. 1: 12; 9: 5; Gal. 2: 11.

55. Preparing the way for 8: 14?

56. See below, pp. 33f., 69f., *et al.*

57. On the sending in pairs, see J. Jeremias, 'Paarweise Sendung im Neuen Testament', *New Testament Essays: Studies in Memory of T. W. Manson*, ed. by A. J. B. Higgins (Manchester 1959), pp. 136-43.

58. Cf. C. H. Dodd, 'The Framework of the Gospel Narrative', reprinted in *New Testament Studies* (Manchester 1953), pp. 1-11. In his translation of the Marcan *Sammelberichte*, in which he emphasizes the imperfect tenses, Dodd renders, 'And He summons the Twelve and began to send them out two by two; and He used to give them authority over foul fiends; and they went out and preached repentance. They kept expelling many demons and anointing

many sick folk with oil and healing them. And the apostles gather to Jesus and reported to Him all that they had done and said' (p. 8). He adds: 'The outline gives a conspectus of the Galilæan Ministry in three stages. . . . C. Retirement in the Hill-country with a small circle of disciples, who are sent on preaching and healing tours' (ibid.; note the plural, *tours*).

59. See J. Jeremias, *Jesus' Promise to the Nations*, Studies in Biblical Theology **24** (London 1958); cf. D. Borsch, *Die Heidenmission in der Zukunftsschau Jesu*, Abhandlungen zur Theologie des Alten und Neuen Testaments **36** (Zürich 1959); also S. G. Wilson, 'Gentiles and Gentile Mission in Luke-Acts' (Durham dissertation 1969).

60. C. K. Barrett, 'Cephas and Corinth', *Abraham unser Vater: Festschrift für Otto Michel*, ed. by O. Betz, M. Hengel, and P. Schmidt (Leiden/Köln 1963), pp. 1–12.

61. For a recent survey of the traditional and archaeological material, see O. Cullmann, *Petrus: Jünger–Apostel–Märtyrer* (Zürich/Stuttgart 1960); Eng. trans. by Floyd V. Filson: *Peter: Disciple, Apostle, Martyr* (2nd edn, revised, London 1962). H. Lietzmann's *Petrus und Paulus in Rom* (Bonn 1915) is still not to be neglected.

62. This is not the only way in which Revelation understands the term 'apostle'; see below, pp. 6of.

63. The translation of Gal. 1:19 is uncertain. It can be rendered, 'I saw no other of the apostles except James', or 'I saw no other of the apostles, but I did see James'. See the commentaries.

64. In Philippians, and in 1 and 2 Thessalonians, Paul is joined by others, and perhaps for this reason avoided the word 'apostle', though indeed the same fact did not prevent him from using it in 1 and 2 Corinthians. It is possible that 1 and 2 Thessalonians were too early, and Philippians was too late, for the question, Who may legitimately claim to be an apostle?, to have any controversial interest.

65. See my article 'ΨΕΥΔΑΠΟΣΤΟΛΟΙ (2 Cor. 11:13)', *Mélanges offerts au Révérend Père Béda Rigaux*, ed. by A. de Halleux, (Gembloux 1970), pp. 377–96.

66. Still the most illuminating discussion is, in my view, Käsemann's 'Legitimität (see no. 17). See also my 'Christianity at Corinth', *Bulletin of the John Rylands Library* **46** (1964), pp. 269–97. I hope to return to the discussion in a commentary. For other views, which I cannot here discuss, see D. Georgi, *Die Gegner des Paulus im 2. Korintherbrief*, Wissenschaftliche Monographien zum Alten und Neuen Testament **11** (Neukirchen 1964) and G. Friedrich, 'Die Gegner des Paulus im 2. Korintherbrief', in *Abraham* (as in n. 60), pp. 181–215.

67. οἱ δοκοῦντες; 6:3 ('If anyone *has a name* for being something when he is nothing, he deceives himself') makes it probable that there is at least a hint, and probably a good deal more than a hint, of irony in the expression. See my 'Paul and the "Pillar" Apostles', *Studia Paulina in honorem J. de Zwaan*, ed. by J. N. Sevenster and W. C. van Unnik (Haarlem 1953), pp. 1–19.

68. οἱ δοκοῦντες στῦλοι εἶναι.

69. ψευδάδελφοι; this word is discussed in the article mentioned in n. 65, pp. 377ff.

70. In the light of the epistle as a whole this must be the meaning of ἵνα ἡμᾶς καταδουλώσουσιν, 'that they might enslave us'. The 'us' shows how closely Paul identified himself with the Gentile churches; it is evident from the sequel that Peter did not do this.

71. Gal. 1:19. It is uncertain (see n. 63) whether this verse implies that James was thought of as an apostle; but it is noteworthy that in Gal. 2:9 his name heads the list.

72. The rendering is uncertain; see n. 63.

73. See pp. 46f.

74. Even if they had seen him, as they may well have claimed, and rightly, they had misunderstood and mis-

represented him, and were in this sense preaching 'another Jesus' (2 Cor. 11:4), and exposing themselves to the curse that not even an angel could escape if he preached a different Gospel (Gal. 1:8).

75. For this element in Paul's definition of an apostle see further below, pp. 41–46.

76. Cf. Käsemann, 'Legitimität' (n. 17), who thinks that the Jerusalem apostles were not *directly* responsible for the Corinthian intruders. 'The primitive apostles (*Urapostel*) have their place in the middle of the battle that is being fought, even though their names appear only in a shadowy way. Their shadow itself is sufficient to constrain Paul to the stiffest resistance. It became his care not to bring them any more clearly into the picture, because only so could he keep a free hand against his Corinthian adversaries. Perhaps one might formulate the matter thus: He defends himself against the primitive apostles, and attacks (*schlägt*) the intruders in Corinth' (p. 48; p. 30 of the reprint).

77. See below, pp. 69–73.

78. Especially 2 Cor. 3:1; 10:12, 18. Cf. also 4:2; 5:12; 6:4; 12:11; which imply that others sought and used commendations, as Paul did not. Paul wrote a commendation for Phoebe (Rom. 16:1).

79. See Schweizer (as in n. 17), 23 e.

80. 2 Cor. 12:12: τὰ σημεῖα τοῦ ἀποστόλου. The addition of τέρατα and δυνάμεις shows that miracles are at least included in what is meant; but note the context in which the miracles are placed. To appeal to them is part of that folly in which Paul permits himself to indulge in this chapter. Cf. Käsemann, 'Legitimität' (as in n. 17), especially p. 63 (pp. 53f. of the reprint).

81. *The Apostle and his Message* (as in n. 11), p. 3.

82. See Rom. 9–11, especially 11:13f., 23, 25–32; J. Munck, *Christ and Israel, An Interpretation of Romans 9—11* (Philadelphia 1967).

83. A common feature of Jewish apocalyptic is the belief

that suffering for the people of God will increase and rise to a climax immediately before God establishes his kingdom. See, for example, W. Bousset, *Die Religion des Judentums im späthellenistischen Zeitalter* (3rd edn, ed. H. Gressmann, Tübingen 1926), pp. 250f.

84. *Annales* 15. 44.

85. The material, such as it is, is surveyed by Rengstorf (nn. 1, 2), von Campenhausen (n. 12), and Mosbech (n. 13).

86. ἀπόστολος Χριστοῦ ʼΙησοῦ: 1 Cor. 1: 1; 2 Cor. 1: 1; Col. 1: 1; cf. 1 Thess. 2: 7.

87. Cf. P. Bachmann, *Der erste Brief des Paulus an die Korinther* (4th edn., with supplements by E. Stauffer; Leipzig 1936), pp. 33f.: 'This genitive is, however, no mere genitive of possession, but names Jesus Christ as at the same time the originator of the apostleship that came into being through calling, and also as the cause of the calling that called it forth.'

88. Rom. 1: 1; Gal. 1: 10; Phil. 1: 1; cf. Col. 4: 12.

89. Rom. 11: 13.

90. Cf. also Paul's anxiety always to act as a pioneer: Rom. 15: 20; 2 Cor. 10: 13ff.

91. See n. 82.

92. See pp. 44f.

93. Rom. 16: 7. The clause could be translated: 'who are men of note in the eyes of the apostles', but it is much more probable that it means: 'who are men of note among the apostles'.

94. Alternatively the plural could be taken as equivalent to a singular: *I* might have acted as *an apostle* of Christ. C. Masson (*Les deux Épitres de Saint Paul aux Thessaloniciens* [Neuchâtel/Paris 1957], p. 28) notes that Paul never gave the title 'apostle' to Timothy, and therefore hesitates to take the plural as a real plural – 'apostles'. But most other commentators seem to take it this way.

95. More accurately, eleven; but the sequel shows that

Luke believed that there were other witnesses of the resurrection (Acts 1 : 22).

96. The MS D oddly has, 'with the ten apostles'.

97. They are distinguished from, though associated with, 'the multitude of those who believed' (verse 32).

98. See K. H. Rengstorf, 'Die Zuwahl des Matthias', *Studia Theologica* **15** (1962), pp. 35–67; there is a shortened English version in *Current Issues in New Testament Interpretation: Essays in honor of Otto A. Piper*, ed. by W. Klassen and G. F. Snyder (New York 1962), pp. 178–92.

99. Rengstorf is right in arguing that the significance of the number is eschatological and relates to the mission to Israel, and is neither mystical nor Qumranite.

100. Op cit., p. 192 (English); there is no precise equivalent in the German.

101. See below, p. 53.

102. In the German edition Rengstorf notes this point: the significance of the event of Pentecost runs deep; 'this is shown by the fact that the Twelve do not simply disappear with the coming of the Spirit, but that the Spirit rather takes them into his service (Acts 2 : 14, 37), even if, as a college, only for quite a short time (cf. Acts 6 : 2)' (p. 65).

103. The literature on this subject is extensive. See E. Haenchen, *Die Apostelgeschichte* (Göttingen 1965), pp. 218–22.

104. A. Harnack, *The Acts of the Apostles* (London 1909), p. 118. Harnack also says (loc. cit.): 'On the whole the book makes St. Paul stand out in ever so much clearer light than St. Peter—at the conclusion the reader possesses quite a distinct portrait of the former apostle, while St. Peter as a *personality* is of a shadowy, and indeed a somewhat conventional type.' This is true, but it would be wrong to conclude, without further consideration, that the portrait of Paul must be historical simply because it is distinct.

105. See, for example, Haenchen, *Apg.*, pp. 99–103; P. Vielhauer, in *Studies in Luke–Acts: Essays presented in*

honor of P. Schubert (London 1968), ed. by L. E. Keck and J. L. Martyn, pp. 33–50. Vielhauer sums up (p. 48): 'The author of Acts is in his Christology pre-Pauline, in his natural theology, concept of the law, and eschatology, post-Pauline. He presents no specifically Pauline idea.'

106. C. K. Barrett, *Luke the Historian in Recent Study* (Philadelphia 1970), p. 70, n. 78: 'That is, an admirer of Paul; one who takes his part, and reproduces his doctrinal system, not perfectly, but as well as he is able.' Haenchen and Vielhauer agree that Luke was an admirer of Paul.

107. U. Wilckens, in *Studies in Luke–Acts* (as in n. 105), p. 77.

108. Wilckens, op. cit., p. 76, quoting E. Dinkler.

109. H. Flender, *St Luke, Theologian of Redemptive History* (London 1967). See especially pp. 163–7.

110. The framework of Paul's mind and thought remained Jewish, as W. D. Davies has repeatedly and rightly emphasized; but 1 Cor. 9: 19ff. betray a radically non-Jewish attitude.

111. See my article 'ΨΕΥΔΑΠΟΣΤΟΛΟΙ' in the Rigaux Festschrift (see n. 65), pp. 385, 387. These two extraordinary things are seldom, I believe, given full weight by students of early Christianity.

112. Not only witnesses of the resurrection; Acts 1: 21f.; 10.37ff. This is for Luke a point of some importance.

113. *Luke the Historian* (as in n. 106), p. 72, n. 82: 'It is vital to Luke's purpose . . . to show that the whole Christian mission sprang from the work of Jesus, and . . . he does this by introducing a connection between each missionary development and the Jerusalem church. It is a historical not an ecclesiastical device that he employs. . . .'.

114. K. Barth's description: *The Epistle to the Romans* (Oxford 1933), p. 258.

115. Their author, too, was a Paulinist (see n. 106), and his purposes were similar to Luke's. See C. F. D. Moule, *The Birth of the New Testament* (London 1962), pp. 220f.

116. See my commentary on the Pastoral Epistles in the New Clarendon Bible (Oxford 1963), pp. 15–18.

117. G. Friedrich, in *Theologisches Wörterbuch zum Neuen Testament* **3**, p. 695. Further, as Friedrich adds, in the New Testament the κηρύσσειν (heralding, proclamation, preaching) is more important than the κῆρυξ (herald, preacher).

118. See P. N. Harrison, *The Problem of the Pastoral Epistles* (Oxford 1921), pp. 126–35; *Paulines and Pastorals* (London 1964), pp. 117–28.

119. The writer continues, 'That in me first Jesus Christ might show all his longsuffering, as an example for those who were to believe in him.' That is, the apostle is a sort of microcosm of the church – a not un-Pauline thought, though Paul does not express it in this way.

120. Marcion was a second-century heretic who rejected the Old Testament and regarded Paul as the only true apostle of Christ.

121. See below, pp. 75ff.

122. For the doctrine of the ministry in the Pastorals, not discussed here, see my commentary (as in n. 116), pp. 29–32, and on the relevant passages.

123. Since apostles are mentioned first, it is probable that Christian prophets, not Old Testament prophets, are in mind.

124. Cf. Matt. 16: 17: 'Flesh and blood did not reveal it to you, but my Father who is in heaven.'

125. That these missionary apostles continued, at least in some quarters, till a much later period is probably to be concluded from the reference to such persons in the *Didache*, a document written probably – its date is disputed – towards the end of the first century.

126. See below, p. 75.

127. For the translation, see H. Windisch, *Die katholischen Briefe*, Handbuch zum Neuen Testament **15** (3rd edn, ed. by H. Preisker, Tübingen 1951), pp. 98ff.

128. Note Marcion's exaggerated Paulinism (n. 120), and Valentinus' use of the Pauline letters.

129. For the problems raised by 2 Peter, see especially E. Käsemann, 'Eine Apologie der urchristlichen Eschatologie', *Exegetische Versuche und Besinnungen I* (Göttingen 1960), pp. 135–57; Eng. trans. by W. J. Montague: *Essays on New Testament Themes*, Studies in Biblical Theology **41** (London 1964), Chapter VIII, pp. 169–95.

130. See below, pp. 74ff.

131. Cf. the 'false apostles' Paul refers to in 2 Cor. 11: 13; see above, pp. 36ff.

132. The Greek *apostolos* is a verbal noun derived from the verb *apostellein*, to send.

133. See above, pp. 24f.

134. See, above all, E. C. Hoskyns, *The Fourth Gospel* (ed. by F. N. Davey; London 1940); the whole of the Introduction, but especially pp. 93–126.

135. Hardly Revelation; though no book could stress more forcibly the fundamental importance of 'the twelve apostles of the Lamb' (21: 14).

136. It is perhaps the one unsatisfactory feature of Westcott's theological approach to the gospel that he links apostolicity inseparably with authorship, making it a purely literary and not a theological issue.

137. Neither C. H. Dodd (*Bulletin of the John Rylands Library* **21** [1937], pp. 129–56) nor W. F. Howard (*Journal of Theological Studies* **48** [1947], pp. 12–25; reprinted in *The Fourth Gospel in Recent Criticism and Interpretation* [London 1955], pp. 282–96), to name only two of the most notable debaters, can be said to have proved his case conclusively.

138. The clumsy construction of the sentence is responsible for a number of variant readings, as well as for the awkward English of the text, which nevertheless probably represents with sufficient accuracy what John wrote.

139. In this, John is at one with Paul and Acts – and, for that matter, with the rest of the New Testament.

140. It will be important later to recall this fact; see below, pp. 111f.

141. Thus, in Mark he is addressed as 'Rabbi' (three or four times), or 'Teacher' (ten times) – not theologically loaded titles that Christological interest would have been inclined to introduce into the tradition.

142. C. K. Barrett, *Jesus and the Gospel Tradition* (London 1967), pp. 28f.

143. T. W. Manson, *Teaching* (as in n. 50), pp. 237–40, suggests that the disciples were not *pupils* (as in rabbinic schools) but *apprentices*. 'Their work was not study but practice' (p. 239).

144. See above, pp. 31–5.

145. The disciples of a rabbi would perform services for him as well as learning from him; e.g. Berakoth 7b.

146. See pp. 30f., and n. 50.

147. See pp. 77f.

148. Hints in Acts lead from the appointment of the Seven to the dispersion of Christians (but not of the apostles, 8: 1) from Jerusalem, and thus to the evangelizing of Samaria (8: 4, 5), of the Ethiopian eunuch (8: 26ff.), and of Antiochene Gentiles (11: 19, 20).

149. Acts 11: 20.

150. It may well be that Peter did not understand ἀπόστολος (*shaliaḥ*) in the same way as Paul. To Paul it meant 'missionary'; to Peter, with the Jewish usage of *shaliaḥ* in his mind, it may have meant primarily 'agent', in the sense of 'administrator' – he was the 'administrator' of the Jewish Christian communities. Such a difference in usage could have been a fruitful source of misunderstanding and dispute.

151. For Jews in such surroundings, see V. Tcherikover, *Hellenistic Civilization and the Jews* (Philadelphia 1959), pp. 269–377, as well as the older works of E. Schürer and J. Juster.

152. See above, pp. 41–4, and below, pp. 93f.

153. See *Studia Paulina* (as in n. 67), pp. 13f.

154. See above, p. 36f.

155. See n. 150.

156. See above, pp. 57f.

157. The tradition is not unanimous, and faces the problem of the silence of Ignatius and others who might have been expected to refer to the presence of John in Ephesus but do not do so. The alternative tradition of the martyrdom of John at the hands of Jews would equally have the effect of removing John from the scene in Jerusalem.

158. If 'all the apostles' are to be distinguished from 'the twelve'. See pp. 46f.

159. 1 Cor. 9: 6 implies that Barnabas shared with Paul (but, like Paul, did not use) the right to be supported at the church's expense. Cf. 1 Thess. 2: 7, where it is not easy to be certain how the plural should be interpreted; see n. 94.

160. Cf. Acts 14: 4, 14; also 14: 12.

161. See e.g. Rom. 3: 8; 6: 1, 15; 7: 7; 14: 1—15: 13; 15: 30f.; 16: 17f.; Phil. 1: 15ff.; 3: 2–11, 18f.; Col. 2: 16f., 20ff.

162. In the New Testament see 2 Tim. 4: 6ff. Later tradition begins with 1 Clem. 5: 5ff., and from this time the fact of Paul's martyrdom does not seem to have been doubted.

163. In the New Testament see John 21: 18f. 1 Clement (5: 3f.) sets Peter with Paul. See also the literature cited in n. 61.

164. See Josephus, *Antiquities* 20. 200; Eusebius, *Church History* ii, 23, 3–18 (cited from Hegesippus).

165. See n. 157.

166. This fact, though undoubtedly in itself a problem, may have helped to secure a solution. The future of the people of God, and the relation within it of Jews and Gentiles, had to be re-thought, and the re-thinking had to proceed on missionary lines. This must have worked in favour of Paul's conception of apostolicity.

167. See p. 54.

168. See pp. 57f.

169. See p. 33.

170. See below, pp. 97–103, and my article, 'The Apostles in and after the New Testament', *Svensk Exegetisk Årsbok* **21** (1956), pp. 30–49.

171. Heretics are not to be allowed to argue their case on the basis of the Scriptures; the Scriptures do not belong to them, and they have no right to use them. The *petitio principii* needs no pointing out.

172. For the gnostics generally, see below, pp. 97–103.

173. It is worth noting that even the most ecclesiastically inclined documents show no interest in establishing a formal succession from the apostles as the basis of the church's apostolicity.

174. I use the personal name to stand for the whole Johannine corpus, whether written by one person or several.

175. Some have found an idealized portrait of Paul in the 'disciple whom Jesus loved'. See n. 34.

176. See p. 67.

177. See pp. 21–31.

178. Cf. Luke 9: 10 ('the apostles returned') with 10: 17 ('the seventy returned').

179. For details, see Strack and Billerbeck, op. cit., **I**, pp. 738–41.

180. That is, of *halakah*.

181. Not, as the saying is sometimes taken to mean, to the Twelve as a group. They are 'disciples' (18: 1) who are addressed, and the promises of 18: 19f. are addressed to any groups of Christians, however small.

182. See pp. 31f., 69f.

183. It is clear on textual and other grounds that Mark 16: 9–20 was not written by the author of the rest of the book, but was a supplement designed to complete what was, or appeared to be, an unfinished book.

184. Viz. Q. It is not important here to inquire whether Q (the non-Marcan material common to Matthew and Luke) was a single written source; in this verse Matthew and Luke are in very close agreement.

185. The Lucan form (Luke 22: 25f.) is later; it presupposes the existence of rulers in the church. This was a necessary and inevitable development; a society can hardly exist without officials. What is important is that when these arose, the teaching of Jesus was recognized to be decisive for their behaviour.

186. It is important to compare this Matthean chapter with the parallels in Mark and Luke. Undoubtedly it is a discourse that has been editorially developed out of various sources. The details cannot be traced in this note, but it should be observed that though in the early Christian tradition forces were at work that tended to exalt church officials and bestow honorific titles upon them, a tendency in the opposite direction, derived from the earliest days, continued to be operative.

187. And therefore not simply created under Pauline influence.

188. I cannot here examine the origin of this material. Its originator was Jesus, though not necessarily in the sense that he spoke all the words attributed to him. Paul learned from him, though perhaps rather from the fact of his death than from any recorded utterances of his.

189. We know the beginning but not the end of the conflicts in Antioch, Galatia, and Corinth. It has often been supposed that Paul was defeated at least in Antioch, and had to relinquish practical interest in the church there. The plainest, though not the profoundest, indication of his final victory is that the Twelve are described in terms of Paul – even if of a Paul somewhat superficially understood.

190. It is not easy, for example, to see how traditions of Jesus' words, memorized rabbinic fashion, and sayings

that envisaged a different end for the ministry, could pass through such events unscathed.

191. See pp. 36–40.

192. The theme is taken up in 1 Tim. 1: 13, and was perhaps regarded by some as the great proof of Paul's apostleship. He himself refers to his interrupted career as a persecutor not frequently but at important points: 1 Cor. 15: 9; Gal. 1: 13, 23; Phil. 3: 6. Gal. 1: 15 suggests the call of a prophet (cf. Jer. 1: 5), but Paul does not often use this kind of language.

193. 1 Cor. 15: 8: 'one born out of due season'.

194. Cf. 2 Cor. 13: 5: 'Test yourselves, to see if you are in the faith; try yourselves.'

195. 'From James' (Gal. 2: 12) must mean 'sent by James'.

196. 2 Cor. 12: 12. Various interpretations of the verse have been given, but it seems certain that miracles are in mind. See n. 80.

197. Since none of those present has left a record of the proceedings.

198. Mark 3: 22; it is worth noting that the allegation shows that the adversaries of Jesus believed him to be capable of supernatural – or, as they might have said, infranatural – acts of power.

199. See E. Käsemann, 'Die Gegenwart des Gekreuzigten', in *Christus Unter Uns*, ed. by F. Lorenz (Berlin 1967), pp. 5–18.

200. The fact of this variety ought not to need demonstration at this time of day; see, e.g., B. H. Streeter, *The Primitive Church* (London 1929), p. ix: 'Everyone has won, and all shall have prizes.' But the variety is not best expressed by saying that episcopacy, presbyterianism, and independency can all be found in the New Testament. The fact is that in the New Testament there is nothing remotely resembling twentieth-century episcopacy; and twentieth-century presbyterianism and independency do not fare much better (though they do fare better). It is

worth while here to recall some of the findings of the Methodist Conference of 1746:

'Q. Why is it, that there is no determinate plan of church government appointed in Scripture?

'A. Without doubt, because the wisdom of God had a regard to this necessary variety.'

201. Mark 9: 38–41; cf. Acts 10, 11 – with Wesley's note on 11.17: 'And *who are* we, *that we should withstand* God? Particularly by laying down Rules of Christian Communion, which exclude any whom he has admitted into the Church of the First-born, from worshipping God together. O that all Church-Governors would consider, how bold an usurpation this is, on the Authority of the supreme Lord of the Church! O that the Sin of thus *withstanding* God, may not be laid to the charge of those, who perhaps with a Good intention, but in an over-fondness for their own Forms, have done it, and are continually doing it!'

202. I hope I need not say that when I used these words I was thinking of the Westminster Confession, not of the headquarters of British Methodism!

203. Jesus reaffirmed the elemental Old Testament faith in God: Deut. 6: 4f., quoted in Mark 12: 29f. (and parallels). What is meant here are the propositions on which Jewish orthopraxy was based.

204. Cf. Matt. 11: 25 = Luke 10: 21: 'I thank thee, Father, Lord of heaven and earth, that thou didst hide these things from the wise and intelligent, and didst reveal them to babes.'

205. Mark describes those who receive the secret of the kingdom of God as οἱ περὶ αὐτόν, 'those who were about him' (4: 10), which he can hardly have failed to understand in terms of 3: 34f.

206. Sometimes not even this was asked for as a condition for a miracle; e.g. Mark 5: 1–20; and the feeding miracles, Mark 6: 35–43; 8: 1–10.

207. John 9: 35; 11: 25ff. represent a late stage in the tradition, in which it was perceived – rightly – that confidence in Jesus calls for some kind of intellectual (and that means Christological) expression.

208. The 'sinners' of the gospels are, for the most part, the *'am ha-'aretz*, the people of the land, who did not observe the law as understood by the Pharisees.

209. I do not mean that no Christological formulation is possible or desirable; see n. 207. The emphasis is on the word 'exclusive'. The supreme example of what Christians ought *not* to say is the *Quicunque Vult* (or 'Athanasian Creed'), which attaches to a quantity of fourth- and fifth-century technical Christological formulas the statement: 'This is the Catholick Faith, which except a man believe faithfully, he cannot be saved.' This is not so.

210. See above, p. 41.

211. 1 Cor. 16: 15–18; Phil. 2: 29; 1 Thess. 5: 11–14. Paul does not impose leaders on the community, but asks for recognition of those who are in fact doing the work. See my commentary on 1 Corinthians, ad loc., and 'The Ministry in the New Testament', in *The Doctrine of the Church*, ed. by Dow Kirkpatrick (New York 1964), pp. 48f.

212. See, e.g., the treatment of the ἄτακτοι ('disorderly') at Thessalonica (1 Thess. 5: 14; 2 Thess. 3: 6, 11); Paul's desire that things should be done 'decently and in order' at Corinth (1 Cor. 14: 40); the praise of good order at Colossae (Col. 2: 5).

213. 'Jesus is Lord' (Rom. 10: 9; 1 Cor. 12: 3) is much more an expression of loyalty than a creed, though creeds (which serve other purposes) may be, and have been, legitimately derived from it.

214. Note 1 Cor. 15: 1–11, which sums up the teaching Paul had received ('Christ died for our sins according to the Scriptures, he was buried, he was raised on the third day according to the Scriptures'), and concludes: 'Whether it was I or they, so we preach and so you believed.'

215. The context is worth quoting more fully. 'He to whom preaching is not denied is also worthy of the Supper, so far as he does not himself refuse it. For Christ comes to the godless, even on Sunday morning. The fact that he does come to us puts an end to godlessness, and makes men worthy. Otherwise we are erecting in the midst of Protestantism an absolutely godless and unworthy system of dependence on works (*Werkerei*)' (E. Käsemann, *Der Ruf der Freiheit* [3rd edn, Tübingen 1968], p. 68). Cf. the English translation, *Jesus Means Freedom* (SCM, London 1969), p. 52.

216. Cf. Wesley's sermon *Catholic Spirit*.

217. Note that Paul makes no attempt to put down Corinthian dissidence ('I am of Cephas' etc.) by the exercise of authority, and that he can rejoice when Christ is preached even out of envy and strife, and with personal ill-will directed against himself (Phil. 1:15–18).

218. E.g. the offender of 1 Cor. 5:1. To behave in this way offends against love – a principle which involves not a less but a more stringent code of sexual ethics than the Ten Commandments. Not all modern writers on ethics appear to have noticed this.

219. 1 Cor. 5:5: 'that his spirit may be saved in the day of the Lord.'

220. 1 Cor. 16:22; see the note in my commentary. It is reasonable to infer that 'all who love the Lord' may properly be invited to the Lord's Supper.

221. See Rom. 15:25–28; 1 Cor. 16:1–4; 2 Cor. 8, 9. The words Paul uses are striking: not only λογεία, but κοινωνία, χάρις, διακονία.

222. The motivation of the collection has been much discussed. See D. Georgi, *Die Geschichte der Kollekte des Paulus für Jerusalem*, Theologische Forschung, Wissenschaftliche Beiträge zur kirchlich-evangelischen Lehre **38** (Hamburg–Bergstedt 1965); K. F. Nickle, *The Collection*, Studies in Biblical Theology **48** (London 1966). Whatever other

motives may have played a part, it would be hard not to see in the collection an act of Christian love and service to the needy.

223. The account in Acts 6:1 reflects Jewish customs of caring for the poor; see the commentaries.

224. 1 Cor. 12:29. Probably some in Corinth would have been ready to answer Yes, thereby claiming every possible Christian privilege for themselves, and showing an understanding of apostleship that Paul did not share. Christians may have 'equal' shares in the church's mission without possessing identical gifts.

225. See above, pp. 80f.

226. 2 Cor. 4.10; cf. pp. 42f.

227. 'Servant of the servants of God'; *servus etiam eorum qui servi Dei non sunt*, 'servant also of those who are not God's servants', would be a healthy addition.

228. The title seems to have been applied to the bishop of Rome first under Gregory the Great, and became customary from the time of Gregory VII; the story of Canossa (where the Emperor Henry IV in 1077 waited three days, a barefooted penitent in the snow, for absolution at Gregory's hands) is an interesting comment on it.

229. Perhaps the story of Gregory and Henry can be accommodated here – with a stretch.

230. Mark 15:34. Attempts to give this saying a different meaning have a touch of Docetism about them. See *Jesus and the Gospel Tradition* (as in n. 142), pp. 48, 107f. To say this is not to say that Jesus did not believe in and predict his future vindication – or that the Christian does not share in the confident hope of God's final victory.

231. With the exception of James. This is the point of Luther's complaint against the Epistle. What can this virtuous tract of a good pious man be but an epistle of straw, if it does not preach Christ? See p. 113. Modern attempts to rehabilitate James *on this issue* seem to me to come near to special – and unconvincing – pleading.

232. It has been said that 'the gospels grew backwards', that is, it was found that a narrative of the passion needed narrative and teaching material to introduce it and make it intelligible.

233. B. L. Manning, *A Layman in the Ministry* (London 1942), p. 138.

234. See pp. 35–40.

235. E.g. 1 Cor. 9: 1f.; 2 Cor. 10: 7–11.

236. That is, by Paulinists whose developing ecclesiastical interests led them to see Paul and his work in a new light; also by gnosticizing and antinomian Paulinists.

237. See 'The Apostles in and after the New Testament' (as in n. 170), which I draw on here because it will be inaccessible to many readers.

238. The best introduction to the subject is R. McL. Wilson, *Gnosis and the New Testament* (Oxford 1968). I do my best to observe his distinction between gnosticism (the Christian heresy) and gnosis, a phenomenon independent of Christianity.

239. The θεῖος ἀνήρ; usually a travelling philosopher and miracle-worker, believed by his followers to have supernatural powers and to be in some sense divine.

240. Though this is not fair to all gnostics. For a philosophical analysis of gnosis see H. Jonas, *Gnosis und spätantiker Geist* (Göttingen 1954). The gnostics in general were not mere spinners of fairy tales, but entertained a serious (even if mistaken) view of the universe and of man's place within it.

241. This thumbnail sketch suffers greatly from over-simplification. In particular I leave aside the question of the date at which, and the means by which, the figure of the Redeemer-Revealer entered the world of gnosis.

242. 'He whose desires are drawn towards knowledge in every form will be absorbed in the pleasures of the soul, and will hardly feel bodily pleasure – I mean, if he be a true philosopher and not a sham one' (Plato, *Republic* VI, 485 D). See also W. Windelband, *History of Ancient Philosophy*

(London 1956), p. 193: 'The fundamental principle of the metaphysical epistemology of Plato is this: TWO WORLDS must be distinguished, one of which *is* and never *becomes*, the other of which *becomes* and never *is*; one is the object of the reason (νόησις), the other is the object of sense (αἴσθησις). . . . . *A rational theory of knowledge requires an immaterialistic metaphysics.*' The marks of emphasis are Windelband's (and his translator's).

243. See Wilson (as in n. 238).

244. On second-century gnosticism see below, pp. 97–103: for Marcion also n. 120.

245. A Valentinian gnostic work discovered at Nag Hammadi in 1946–7. It goes back to the middle of the second century; it has been suggested that it was an early writing of Valentinus himself.

246. A – more or less – orthodox Christian gnostic. 'Clement readily accepts the slogan of the time and of his opponents, and is willing to become a gnostic himself and teach gnosticism, but a gnosticism proper to the church and drawn from the Bible' (H. Lietzmann, *The Founding of the Church Universal* [London 1938], pp. 383f.).

247. Cf. my Delitzsch Lectures, *Das vierte Evangelium und das Judentum*, (Stuttgart 1970) Ch. 4, n. 29.

248. B. Gärtner, *The Theology of the Gospel of Thomas* (London 1961), p. 78.

249. See 'The Apostles in and after the New Testament' (as in n. 170), pp. 34–7. In the *Excerpta ex Theodoto* Clement of Alexandria gives substantial quotations from the Valentinian Theodotus, with his own comments.

250. Quoted from Epiphanius, *Panarion*, xxxiii, 7.

251. It is by no means easy for the modern scholar who looks back to the second century to distribute the titles 'heretical' and 'orthodox'; it must have been far harder at the time, when the notions of orthodoxy and heresy were taking shape. See W. Bauer, *Rechtgläubigkeit und Ketzerei im ältesten Christentum* (Tübingen 1934).

252. The 'orthodox' canon may well have been an enlarged version of Marcion's. Cf. von Campenhausen, *Die Entstehung der christlichen Bibel* (Tübingen 1968), especially pp. 173–95.

253. An interesting example (Ptolemaeus' interpretation of John, quoted from Irenaeus, *Adv. Haer.* I, viii, 5) will be found in R. M. Grant, *Gnosticism: an Anthology* (London 1961), pp. 182f.

254. See C. H. Turner, 'Apostolic Succession: A. the Original Conception', in *Essays on the Early History of the Church and the Ministry* (London 1918), ed. by H. B. Swete, pp. 95–142, especially 104–8.

255. For the development of legalism as early as the Apostolic Fathers, see T. F. Torrance, *The Doctrine of Grace in the Apostolic Fathers* (Edinburgh 1948).

256. In second-century history nothing is more important than the setting up of canons and preservatives of orthodoxy.

257. I use Luther's phrase without committing myself to precisely his understanding of it.

258. Rather, the disciplined freedom at which Paul aimed; it would be unrealistic to suppose that it was ever fully achieved, even in Paul's own time.

259. That its governors were not infrequently grossly immoral is, though scandalous, of less real importance – and indeed less scandalous – than that a ruling 'spiritual' estate should have been thought to exist.

260. The term was used above, p. 53, and finds some explanation in the present paragraph. It means essentially the understanding of Christianity as the pursuit of the glory of God, rather than an acceptance of God as he chooses to come to men – in the humility of the Cross.

261. *Works*, Weimar Edition, **1**, p. 354.

262. *Works*, ed. cit., **1**, p. 362.

263. Cf. J. S. Whale, *The Protestant Tradition* (Cambridge 1955), pp. 78ff.

264. A. Nygren, *Agape and Eros*, II, 2 (London 1939),

especially pp. 506ff.; but the sentence could properly be said to supply the theme for the whole of Nygren's discussion of Luther's treatment of love.

265. No doubt because it is so uncomfortable a doctrine for Catholics of the old school, and for the catholicizing wing of the Protestant churches.

266. 1 Peter 2:9; Rev. 1:6; 5:10; 20:6 are not the only relevant texts, though they are the most evidently relevant.

267. M. Luther, *Babylonian Captivity: Works*, ed. cit., **6**, p. 566; translation from H. Wace and C. A. Buchheim, *Luther's Primary Works* (London 1883), p. 235.

268. It might in fact make for decency, order, and a sense of responsibility in the Christian society, if the members took it in turn at least to share in the administration and ordering of the sacraments; and this would certainly manifest the general priesthood of all Christians.

269. *Babylonian Captivity: Works*, ed. cit., **6**, p. 567; Wace and Buchheim (as in n. 267), p. 236.

270. Ibid.; Wace and Buchheim (as in n. 267), p. 237.

271. 'Wir sind Bettler, das ist wahr!', Luther's last written words, written on 16 February 1546, two days before his death; quoted, e.g., by H. Boehmer, *Der junge Luther* (Gotha 1925), p. 123.

272. G. Rupp, *The Righteousness of God* (London 1953), p. 46: 'It was indeed a pity that Wesley only skimmed a few hundred pages of Luther'; P. S. Watson, *Let God be God!* (London 1947), pp. 3f.: 'He possessed little or no first-hand knowledge of Luther's teaching, and he was misled by the errors of men whom he imagined, as they imagined themselves, to be faithful exponents of Luther.'

273. See especially F. Hildebrandt, *From Luther to Wesley* (London 1951), an invaluable study of the relation between the Reformation and the Revival.

274. There is some parallelism between the careers of Johann Andreas Rothe and John Wesley, in that both fell

under the spell of Zinzendorf, and subsequently broke away from it. It is not easy to compare poetry in different languages, but hard also not to feel that Wesley's translation is the better hymn. Note the characteristic variation to which S. H. Moore (*Sursum Corda* [London 1956], p. 88) refers: 'It is a masterstroke . . . in translating "Oh abyss, in which through Christ's death all sin is engulfed" ["O Abgrund, welcher alle Sünden durch Christi Tod verschlungen hat!"], to introduce the personal pronoun:

> "Oh Love, Thou bottomless abyss,
> *My* sins are swallowed up in Thee,
> Covered is *my* unrighteousness
> Nor spot of guilt remains on *me*." '

It is fair to add that in Rothe's ten-verse hymn, seven verses contain the first person singular, two more the first person plural; the verse Moore singles out is the only one to contain neither.

275. 2 Cor. 4: 12: see above, p. 43; and note the whole context in 2 Cor. 4.

276. This was remedied to a great extent as a result of the conflicts of the nineteenth century.

277. L. Tyerman, *The Life and Times of the Rev. John Wesley* (London 1871), I, p. 369.

278. This would be the wrong word for Germany in the middle '30s, but it is the right word for England; Hoskyns's translation of Barth's commentary on Romans was published in 1933.

279. K. Barth, *Romans* (as in n. 114), p. x: 'Theology is *ministerium verbi divini*.'

280. I say this primarily, and sorrowfully, of the British Methodist Church. It is no wild exaggeration to add that the main exception is to be found in the Roman Catholic Church.

281. For this theme, see, above all, E. Käsemann, *Der Ruf der Freiheit* (as in n. 215). This small book, which origi-

nated as a *Streitschrift* thrown into a situation not quite the same as that of the English-speaking Christian world, is becoming under revision a miniature Theology of the New Testament, written from a special angle. There is now an English translation, *Jesus Means Freedom* (SCM 1969).

282. Not always, of course, in Paul's terminology. That Jesus was the friend of tax-collectors and sinners is in some respects an even better statement of the doctrine of justification by grace through faith than any Paul hit upon.

283. P. 90, with nn. 217, 218.

284. See von Campenhausen, 'Apostelbegriff' (as in n. 11), p. 123: 'In the last resort, the foundation laid by the apostles must carry the apostles too, and precisely in the judgement of the community, and not vice versa.'

285. Op. cit., p. 124.

286. Op. cit., p. 128. Here von Campenhausen is speaking in the first instance of the church at the end of the second century.

287. See n. 140, and cf. the way in which Käsemann raises this question in regard to 2 Peter; n. 129.

288. This is the point of the objection to the requirement, in the plan for uniting the Church of England and the British Methodist Church, of 'the strictest invariability of episcopal ordination' (*Anglican-Methodist Unity: 2, The Scheme* [London 1968], p. 28). Apart from the fact that this must seem to a Christian reasonably acquainted with the New Testament an odd foundation for the church (for the passage continues: 'Any variation from this practice could not but appear as a breach of a foundation principle on which the two Churches will have come together'), it expressly forbids future reformation of the church's order.

289. 'When [John] Robinson bade the Pilgrim Fathers God speed his memorable last words were—"I charge you, before God and His blessed angels, that you follow me no further than you have seen me follow the Lord Jesus Christ.

If God reveal anything to you by any other instrument of His, be as ready to receive it as you were to receive any truth by my ministry, for I am verily persuaded the Lord hath more truth yet to break forth out of His holy word" ' (H. S. Skeats and C. S. Miall, *History of the Free Churches of England* London (1891), p. 34).

290. In the *Vorreden auf die Episteln an die Ebräer, S. Jakobi und S. Judae.*

Additions and Corrections to the Notes

In a number of cases it is now possible to add references to English translations of works referred to in Professor Barrett's notes on pp. 115–43 and to correct or supplement information there. The listing below is given in terms of his footnote numbers. In many instances a U.S. edition also exists for a volume which he has cited from its British publication (e.g., E. Käsemann, *Jesus Means Freedom* [Philadelphia: Fortress, 1969] in notes 215 and 281); such U.S. editions have not been noted below, however.

1. Eng. trans. by Paul D. Pahl, of K. H. Rengstorf's book, *Apostolate and Ministry: The New Testament Doctrine of the Office of the Ministry* (St. Louis: Concordia, 1969).

2. Eng. trans. by G. W. Bromiley, *Theological Dictionary of the New Testament* (Grand Rapids: Eerdmans), Vol. 1 (1964), pp. 398–447, "*apostellō,* etc.," by K. H. Rengstorf.

6. Eng. trans. (cited above, note 1), Rengstorf, *Apostolate,* p. 41.

12. The article by von Campenhausen is in the volume indicated of *Studia Theologica.* Eng. trans. of his book by J. A. Baker, *Ecclesiastical Authority and Spiritual Power in the Church of the First Three Centuries* (Stanford, Calif.: Stanford University Press, 1969).

13. The research report by Mosbech is in the volume indicated of *Studia Theologica,* as is the article by Munck cited in note 14.

16. Eng. trans. by John E. Steely, of Walter Schmithals's book, *The Office of Apostle in the Early Church* (New York & Nashville: Abingdon, 1969).

17. Eng. trans. by Harold Knight, of Jean-Louis Leuba's book, *New Testament Pattern: An Exegetical Inquiry into the "Catholic" and "Protestant" Dualism* (London: Lutterworth, 1953).

52. Eng. trans. by John Marsh, of Rudolf Bultmann's book, *The History of the Synoptic Tradition* (New York: Harper & Row, 1963), p. 145.

103. Eng. trans. by B. Noble and G. Shinn, with H. Anderson and R. McL. Wilson, *The Acts of the Apostles: Commentary* (Phila.: Westminster, 1971), pp. 259–64, with further literature and detailed exegesis, pp. 264–69.

117. Eng. trans., *Theological Dictionary* (cited above, note 2), Vol. 3 (1965), p. 696 (cf. 693 f.).

251. Eng. trans. edited by R. A. Kraft and G. Krodel, *Orthodoxy and Heresy in Earliest Christianity* (Philadelphia: Fortress, 1971).

261. Eng. trans. of the Heidelberg Disputation, by Harold J. Grimm, in *Luther's Works*, Vol. 31, *Career of the Reformer: I*, 3rd ed. rev. (Philadelphia: Fortress, 1971); p. 40: "A theologian of glory calls evil good and good evil. A theologian of the cross calls the thing what it actually is" (Thesis 21).

262. Ibid., p. 53.

290. The Luther quotation is found, in its full context, in the "Preface to the Epistles of Saint James and Saint Jude," 1545 (1522), in the *Works of Martin Luther* (Philadelphia Edition; Philadelphia: Muhlenberg Press, 1932), Vol. 6, p. 478; in *Luther's Works*, Vol. 35, *Word and Sacrament: I* (1960), p. 396.